THREE
PIANOS

THREE PIANOS

Andrew McMahon

A Memoir

PRINCETON ARCHITECTURAL PRESS · NEW YORK

Published by
Princeton Architectural Press
202 Warren Street
Hudson, New York 12534
www.papress.com

ISBN 978-1-64896-020-8

Designer: Paul Wagner

Credits:
"Diane, The Skyscraper," written by Andrew McMahon,
published by Left Here Publishing (ASCAP)/Kobalt Songs Music Publishing (ASCAP);
"Learn To Dance," written by Andrew McMahon, Mark Williams,
published by Left Here Publishing (ASCAP)/Kobalt Songs Music Publishing (ASCAP),
Songs of Kobalt Music Publishing (BMI)

Library of Congress Control Number: 2021939772

For Kelly

Contents

Piano One

1 – Half-Formed Bell ... 13

2 – Lake Effect ... 15

3 – Losing Days in the Ravine ... 23

4 – Fire and the Miracle of Flight ... 27

5 – Don't Bother Unpacking ... 30

6 – The Ghost of South Ardmore ... 32

7 – Saltwater, Birthday, and Two Useful Sets of Wheels ... 44

8 – Some Flowers Grow from Bone ... 55

9 – The Prodigal Father ... 64

10 – Japanese Screens ... 71

11 – Drive-thru Saturday Night ... 79

12 – Young Love, Let's Get Stoned ... 84

13 – The Architect and the Arsonist ... 91

Piano Two

14 – Slingshots at Dawn ... 103

15 – Teenage Rock Star ... 107

16 – Teeth Cutters in the Parking Lot ... 109

17 – Tin Cans, Tires, and Wings ... 114

18 – Glittering Exits ... 121

19 – From the Platform, Launch the Submarine ... 126

20 – Everything in Transit ... 129

21 – Grief for the Living, No Really, I'm Fine ... 132

22 – Walls of Rain ... 136

23 – Dark Blue ... 141

24 – So Long Mr. Invincible ... 147

25 – Women ... 152

26 – Crewcuts and Pneumonia ... 156

27 – The Junk of Blood and Healing ... 161

28 – The Jungle ... 165

29 – Our House in the Trees ... 172

Piano Three

30 – Bulletproof Frankenstein ... 181

31 – The Family You Choose ... 183

32 – The Glass Passenger ... 188

33 – Floating with the Dead ... 202

34 – Tarantula Mating Season ... 206

35 – I Was the Diver, It Was Our World ... 212

36 – People and Things ... 217

37 – The Vampire on Melrose ... 220

38 – New Friends and a Night in Las Vegas ... 223

39 – Wrecking Ball, Rest in Peace ... 228

40 – The Wilderness Years ... 231

41 – Peace in the Desert ... 235

Acknowledgments ... 240

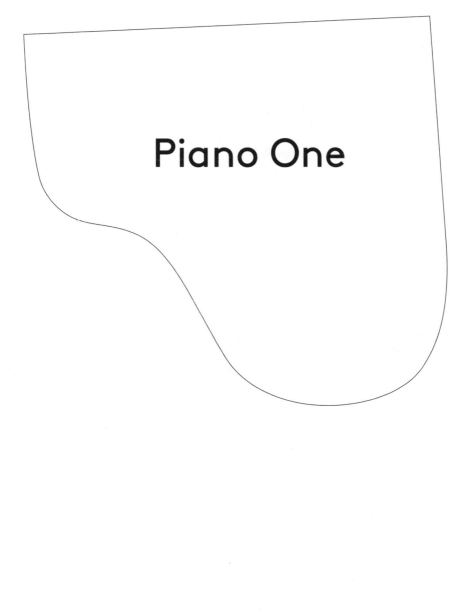

Piano One

The Invention of Sound

The pianoforte was created in the early
1700s by an Italian instrument maker named
Bartolomeo Cristofori, but it took nearly
two hundred years from the time of its invention
for it to become the piano we know today.
A marvel of string, brass, wood, pins, and felt,
with seven playable octaves, made up of more
than ten thousand moving parts. The journey
required countless revisions by makers
the world over in a slow-moving arms race
to perfect what is widely regarded
as humanity's most celebrated instrument.

Chapter 1

Half-Formed Bell

Black satin. Skin like a fun house mirror wrapped around the image of a face—my face. I was six years old, staring you down, the monster in my family's living room. You arrived, a birthday gift for my mother, a symbol of my father's love and a promise of our family's newly acquired station in the North Shore suburbs of Chicago, Illinois. Your checkerboard teeth were not unlike my own, save for the color and the fact that I was missing a few. Every inch of you was an odyssey. The way you curved without reason like a half-formed bell. Your insides, a maze of wire and string fastened to a massive brass plate, a color so disquieting, I would have believed it if I had learned you had been stolen from a pirate's den or the tomb of some great pharaoh. We were alone together like this often, but it would be years before we truly met. At six, time is a slow climb up a roadless mountain. At thirty-eight, it is the psychedelic wash of green from a tree-lined highway through the lens of a camera that can't keep up. We made our pact before those highway years, but, prior to that, you were little more than an oddity with a secret. A fortune-teller out on an extended break. You replaced the spinet, which had lived in the basement of my family's old house in New Jersey. We had just moved from there, and we were now moving up in the world. And like that old brown piano, I was drawn to you and the room where you lived, but I couldn't make you sing the way I dreamed. What I was searching for in those early days was beyond my grasp, but just knowing my hands could raise sound from a resting body was enough for me. By the time you arrived I was becoming a fan of the music filling our home and cars on cross-country road trips. I've loved music for as long as I can remember, and it's that love which found me plucking out the notes to my first favorite songs on your keys in the living rooms of my youth. Looking back, I think I always knew you were the missing piece of me. The key to unlocking worlds and making whole that alien child. Our time would come, but my mother was your first true friend. The Morse code clicking of her fake nails across your keys will forever be married in my mind to the sound of solfeggio and those pieces by the great composers I came to revile during my time in a Midwest conservatory. I don't know how my mother learned to play, but I remember how I felt watching her draw music from the mystery of you. I'd hide myself in some corner of the hall, aching for the magic she possessed. You were hers first, but necessity would bind us together, which made the talk of them selling you, years later, even more insidious and cruel.

♫

Chapter 2

LAKE
EFFECT

My early memories are like pictures of planets captured from outer space. So much color and abstraction; details yielding to epic forms, composed in layers by coordinating eyes. Within those broad strokes, there are fragments that belong to me, self-generated and unchanging with time: the early workings of my own telescoping lens operating free from the machinery of a shared family memory. In that private collection of scenes, you were always nearby. When the shutter stuck or the image failed to develop, somehow you made the frame. In my early blurry life, somewhere just around the corner, were the rooms you so elegantly defined. Your lid propped open upon a narrow arm, an invitation to another world.

♪

Winnetka, Illinois, 1988: I see my family on the front lawn. I'm in the foreground astride a Schwinn bicycle with my sister Kate beside me. My parents, Lin and Brian, and my three older siblings, Emily, Chapman, and Jason, are posed around us. In the background stands the home my parents spent months renovating, a brick masterpiece on the corner of Sheridan Road and Lamson Drive. If you search "happy white family/1980s," I wouldn't be surprised if this image comes up first. The photograph runs with an article in one of those regional magazines that publishes stories about rich people at fundraisers. The article is about my father, the young executive tasked with opening the flagship Chicago store for his employer, a high-end retail chain. He is an impressive man, my dad. He started with the company as a tie salesman and rose through the ranks from buyer to executive in a relatively short time. He married my mother at twenty-eight, becoming a stepfather to my three oldest siblings, an arrangement complicated by the fact that their father drowned while saving them from a tragic boating accident just months before my parents were married. Those details will not make the story. This picture is taken nearly a decade after that tragedy. The chaos of those years does not read in the eyes of the children who survived it. I can't speak to their trauma or how they might have healed from it, but what I know of my own is that confronting the past is not my family's strong suit. Perseverance, on the other hand, is what we know best, that and how to smile for a camera. Even in black-and-white, the image bleeds American idealism, and it would go on to be framed and then hung in every home we inhabited from that day forward. Each one smaller than the last.

When my family moved from New Jersey to the North Shore of Chicago I was six, bucktoothed and dirty blond. A notoriously loud kid, who on at least one occasion was taken to a hearing specialist for concern that I might be partially deaf. According to my mother, the doctor insisted I was fine and not to address the matter, as he felt quite sure some destiny awaited me, and, in it, my voice would play a role. This bit of family folklore began surfacing in conversations shortly after my ninth birthday, when somewhat mysteriously, I sat down at the piano and began writing songs. But I'm less convinced of this gospel now as I weigh its convenience and my mother's ability to spin gold from garbage in the interest of a rich family history.

Compared to my brothers and sisters, I was a peculiar kid. My heroes were Michael Jackson and Phil Collins, and I attended preschool in a rotating uniform of bow ties, sunglasses, penny loafers, and white socks with my jeans cuffed at the bottom. I hated sports, but it took me years to admit it. I can recall at least one occasion sitting in a dugout during a Little League game in the second grade crying to my father because the bat hurt my hands when it made contact with the ball. I had grown accustomed to swinging at air. My teammates must have despised me, but I don't recall thinking too much about popularity until middle school, when I got fat. I can't say with any certainty what caused me to balloon as I eventually did, but it would be easy enough to trace my family's hardest years to the readouts on my scale.

I was born in Concord, Massachusetts, but ended up in Jersey three years later without a single memory of my birthplace to call my own. If life is merely an assemblage of the things we recall, then my life began in Illinois. My family and I were middle-class nomads, a hitched wagon to my father's rising star. Every few years a promotion came in and we packed up the house, said our goodbyes, and started over in the next town.

My father was New Jersey born without the hint of an accent. He was a gentle man with a dark sense of humor, and despite his grueling work schedule, he never felt far away in those early years. He had dark, wavy hair, combed and blow-dried straight each morning, an outward-facing act of deception. I remember being fascinated by an old picture of him from the '60s when he was a stick-thin hippie and wore his hair long. Who was that man? This one was portly, always impeccably dressed and rarely caught without a collared shirt on and neatly pressed pants.

I used to love visiting him at work. When the department store he managed hosted celebrity book signings and public appearances, we got to cut the line and be the first to receive autographs and take pictures. He carried an air of importance with him wherever he went, whether it was a restaurant, a movie theater, or an airplane ride. He was a man in charge, but nowhere was that more apparent than on the floor of his department store. He was the boss; his shine wrapped the whole family, and it was easy to feel like royalty when we stopped in for a visit. The nights he worked late, my father would sneak into the bedroom I shared with Kate, performing puppet shows in the dark until my mother shut him down. I still remember the feeling of falling asleep, my body trembling in the aftershocks of laughter. Even back then, it was clear to me his hard work was responsible for our house on Lake Michigan, the foreign cars in the driveway, and my mother's ability to look after us full-time. But to the best of my recollection, we looked on our good fortune with caution and gratitude, the loss and sacrifice of my oldest siblings' father was enough to level our privilege with humility.

My mother was my best friend growing up. It's well known I was an accident. She tried to name me River after the café where she got loaded with my dad the night I was conceived. Ultimately, they settled on Andrew. In those days, she was vibrant, constantly laughing, and in a house full of children, there was never any question I was her baby, and she had my back. We shared a love of music and long car rides, and I can still see her singing along to the radio with the windows down, the cigarette in her left hand spitting smoke signals into the ether. She gifted my sister and me with her mane of thick blonde hair, a love letter to the California of her youth and the extended family we spent our summers with. She had friends scattered all over the country, a network she'd assembled over years in constant motion, and she passed her time on the kitchen phone with them, shifting through concern and reverie, a pack of Winstons always close by. My early childhood is a slideshow of vacations, moving trucks, soccer games from the bleachers, siblings dressed up for school dances, and my parents dressed up for cocktail parties. Our house was full of teenagers and loose teeth, a circus train with its destination unknown. And at the center of all that chaos and magic, there she was, my mother, the conductor.

Kate was Katie back then, and despite her being eighteen months older than me, we resembled a pair of scrappy twins. Kate was the brains of our operation—I followed her everywhere, and she was my protector. No matter where my sister went those days, a stockpile of security devices traveled with her: a Linus-style blanket, a battered doll named Deedle, and her index finger curled into the shape of a hook, which she gnawed on obsessively. Kate suffered night terrors and slept in my parents' bedroom on and off throughout elementary school. Even in those days, she relied on them in ways I could never make sense of. I was independent, certain I needed no help from anyone, and in one instance, at the age of five, I made it halfway down the street with a packed suitcase, explaining later that I was running off to New York with the neighbor girl. In some ways, Kate and I are very much the same people today.

Winnetka, Illinois, was an ideal place to be a kid. So ideal that it, and the surrounding suburbs of Chicago's North Shore, was the backdrop for John Hughes's iconic films about teenage life in America. I can only imagine what it must have been like for my siblings, Emily and Jason, to come of age in the land of Ferris Bueller and the Breakfast Club. Chapman had already finished high school by then and left for college before we moved. And while those years were less cinematic for me, they've aged well. The remembrance of a childhood. I had the kinds of friends you have when you're a kid. We loved the Simpsons and MTV, taught each other how to curse, and swam in Lake Michigan in the summertime. I wanted for nothing and can recall a day when Kate and I wandered into a toy store with our father and both of us left with new Game Boys; the casual nature of the transaction blew my mind. I knew it meant something, that we had more than we needed. It would not be long before I understood what it meant to have less.

Our early acquaintance was precarious at best, as it was lorded over by a piano teacher whose methods were foreign to me and from whom I learned mostly to fear your company. A true shame, since your unveiling had left me utterly spellbound. When the lessons began, it was Kate who excelled. The scales and shaped notes, the do-re-mis and books of simple songs, made sense to her. I remember feeling disillusioned. I wanted to understand you. When it was clear I could not, I requested a reprieve, and my mother obliged. Kate continued, though I can't say I have any lasting memories of her playing. She confided in me later in life that she quit lessons the day she heard me perform both parts of "Heart and Soul" without requiring her assistance. I didn't know, then, how my days behind your keys might lead to bruises and the occasional burning bridge. If I had though, I doubt I would have changed a thing.

♫

I liked school until the third grade. I doubt I'm the first person to commit those words to a page. I was always the youngest kid in class and probably should have stayed back for an extra year of kindergarten, but I was articulate and imaginative and, at the time, starting elementary school early made sense to everyone, myself included. By third grade, however, it became clear I was struggling to read. I've never been diagnosed with a learning disability and it's possible I was simply in over my head, but my struggle to focus and make sense of the material presented in classrooms would be a source of frustration for the remainder of my days in school. It's around this same time I developed a problem with authority. Not all authority, but my third-grade teacher pushed my buttons, and I got comfortable pushing hers. In one epic bout, she held me after school, and my mother showed up like the fighter I knew her to be, and they had it out while I listened through the door. Mom was always good like that. In hindsight, I was probably humiliated by my inability to follow along. Time would prove me willing to lash out at those tasked with providing me evidence of my shortcomings.

Toward the end of our third and final year in the big house on Sheridan Road, there was a looming sense of dread. In what feels like the simple inhale and exhale of a deep breath, one crisis after another would find and shatter the quiet of otherwise easy days. The first was a car accident in which my sister Emily was badly injured. She would make a full recovery, but, in a family familiar with heartbreak and loss, the repercussions served as a reminder of life's frailty. The second was a prolonged season of joblessness for my father. In the course of three short years, he'd leveraged his success into two failed reinventions, both of which, unbeknownst to me at the time, underscored a new and dangerous pattern of behavior for him: aimless days, depression, and the acceleration of an addiction to opioid pain medication. The third and most pressing crisis, however, was news of our beloved uncle Stuart's rapidly advancing skin cancer.

To speak of my family and not of my uncle Stuart would be like trying to fly an airplane with a missing wing. Like me, he was the baby of his family, and perhaps it was this common thread at the center of our connection. He was my mom's little brother, a visionary entrepreneur and practical joker. He started his first magazine in my grandparents' garage at the age of nineteen, and by thirty he had built a media empire that launched a spandex-clad Jane Fonda into the living rooms of millions of exercising housewives—a move largely responsible for the advent of the home video industry. Stuart's success was an outcropping of his oversized personality, and his presence alone was enough to raise the frequency of a room. Kate and I were close in age with his sons, Cooper and Hamilton, and we spent our summers in California, in awe of their father, swimming in the pool behind their mansion. The news of Stuart's illness was devastating, but its quieting transformation of my mother added a layer to the worry. I was eight years old, and preceding all of this I could be easily offended, was quick to cry, and was often described as hypersensitive. The uncertainty of those days would force my intensity into a spotlight that I channeled into a newfound love of writing. I'd begun my journey inward.

With my father out of work, our only ties to Chicago were school and friends, neither of which carried much water when it came to our survival. My parents decided to relocate to California. Family was everything to my mother, and Stuart was both her brother and the subject of her pride and adulation. We would stay with my grandparents until my father found work and spend Stuart's last days surrounded by cousins, aunts, and uncles preparing for the loss of everybody's favorite someone.

If you were to ask any member of my immediate family, what we left behind in Chicago were our halcyon days. An odd fact considering how short-lived they were and how few memories I would take from that great feast. When school was finished, we packed the house up in brown paper and boxes and began our journey west. My father flew out early to hunt for jobs, and my brothers stayed back with friends for the summer before heading off to college. Meanwhile, my mother, my two sisters, and I drove off in a green Jaguar with enough music to carry us all the way to my grandparents' house on the coast.

You were loaded sideways into an orange semitrailer. Your legs and pedal housing were removed and packed separately, and your body was wrapped in blue packing blankets despite the soaring temperatures of that summer day. This would be your first cross-country move, but certainly not your last.

♫

Chapter 3

Losing Days in the Ravine

The summer of '91 was coming to a close, and everything was changing. The flat, tree-lined streets of suburban Illinois would soon be the sprawling foothills east of Los Angeles. The brick home my parents built from the ground up would be replaced by an ancient, castle-like Tudor on Flintridge Drive. And the simpler days, when loved ones seemed invincible, would end, lost to the memories of hospital goodbyes and a eulogy delivered by my mother, forever altered and choking back tears. It was a month from my ninth birthday when my uncle Stuart, at the age of thirty-eight, lost his battle with cancer.

I slept over at my cousins' house the night their father passed away, waking up to find them both playing Nintendo. Hamilton was six at the time, and with his back to me, and without pausing the game, he broke the news: "Dad died." I wouldn't understand it for years, but he, like most of us, was in shock. For some in my family, I think the shock never fully wore off—namely, my mother and my grandparents. Stuart led a life so big it was hard not to get swept up in it—he made you feel like all his magic belonged to you. His mere existence was the family raft; through him we were buoyant, and all things seemed pos-sible. Without him, we were ships on windless water. The days after his death were lengthy and surreal. I couldn't make sense of my feelings at the time, but there was a heaviness I understand now to be grief.

Prior to that summer, the machinery of death was foreign to me. How to say goodbye to someone in a hospital bed they'll never leave, what to think when those whose strength you've never questioned are reduced to rubble in your company. I remember the wake, how my mother brought us early to view the body because my aunt refused an open casket; I hid a poem in the coffin's satin lining, thinking Stuart might read it when he got to wherever he was going. I remember the short looping mix of songs played on repeat as people filtered in and out, paying their respects. Was I the only one who noticed? At the funeral there was a photograph of Stuart mounted on cardboard and propped up on an easel at the front of the church. When the service was over, I asked if I could keep it, and for the next few years, every bedroom I claimed would be home to a makeshift memorial.

In the end, our weeks' worth of mourning culminated in a party at the house of my mom's older sister and last living sibling, Kristina. There, we watched two videos. One was a collection of photographs and Super 8 movies set to Frank Sinatra's "That's Life." The other, Stuart had recorded in his hospital room. The man whose big ideas played out on sound stages with studio lighting lay ravaged in a land of clicking machines. It seemed to me an unfair ending. Such a stark departing view of a person whose world had been so full of color. If he saw it that way though, he didn't let on. With his eyes fixed on the camera lens, knowing exactly where his gaze would settle, Stuart implored us to stay positive, to take care of one another, and to know there was so much left to look forward to. He was the vision of peace personified, and while it took me years to appreciate the added layer of poetry others might have understood on that day, my uncle chose to say goodbye to us in a home video, the medium he helped invent.

In the weeks leading up to Stuart's passing, my father took a position with a chain of West Coast department stores. We stayed with my grandparents while he worked and searched for a new place for us to live, and on the very night Stuart was buried, we moved into a house in La Cañada, a suburb of Pasadena. The strange castle we briefly called home would become the backdrop to a year of grief and miracles. To reach the house, you traveled a series of labyrinthian streets, and while the address required a steep climb up Flintridge Drive, the house itself sat nearly fifty feet below street level, nestled in the belly of a sprawling ravine. Regardless of the hour, that weird architecture remained subsumed in shadow by a canopy of trees. Why anyone would have chosen to build a house there is beyond me. Perhaps they were hiding from something, and in that way, it suited us well.

The interior was dark. Nearly everything was brown, from the tile on the floor to the carpet in the living room, where in the afternoons the piano sat waiting in one of the few pools of gathering light. The bedrooms were split between the top floor and the basement, which was carved into the heart of the ravine. My sisters and parents claimed the upstairs, and I took one of the two bedrooms on the lower level; the other would be occupied infrequently by my brothers on their visits home from school.

When it got dark, the coyotes came out. Most nights it felt like they were inches from my window, announcing found prey and holding dominion over one of the few remaining wild places within miles of the Pacific. For the first month of nights on Flintridge, I cried myself to sleep under the cover of those coyote songs, praying for Stuart to climb out from the cardboard of his funeral photograph. Then a September day arrived when the grief that had consumed me found its way from my body and into the world.

With my fingertips wandering your double-stacked spine, one vertebra at a time, we began a friendship forged of lost innocence and good medicine. The things I would see too soon, you would help me make sense of, time and again. My uncle was gone, and my life was just beginning.

♫

Chapter 4

Fire and
the Miracle
of Flight

I don't know what brought me there that afternoon. I couldn't tell you if it was a Wednesday or a weekend, but I remember the dark inside the house, and inside my body, a feeling like fire. The fire is what led me to you, but it was the darkness that needed sorting out. I had watched the movers unload you in pieces weeks before, wondering if you'd ever be the same again, but they, like my mother, understood the puzzle of you—the way your first two legs got bolted to your body sideways before they tipped you upright and attached the third. How a tuner's steady hand could bring you back to life after so many violent, humid miles in the dark. There, next to the window, which I remember as a wall of glass, you sat untouched until that afternoon. Outside, infinite shades of green and brown gathered together—an impossible garden. The fir trees and big leaf maples stood guard, but the cloud cover that day made their job an easy one. The air was a void, death was a vacuum, and I filled the emptiness with grief and longing. Somewhere between the fire and the infinite ravine was you. The sentry in our house of mourning. You invited me to keep watch with you that day, and I never left. I sat before you, legs dangling from your bench, feet dreaming of the ground below, adolescence closing in fast. Outside there was basketball and neighbor kids, and down the hall, a television with piss-poor reception always disappointing someone. None of it mattered anymore. I didn't know why, until I made the shape of a chord and heard you speak for the very first time. The chord was a gift from Rick Kertes, my first friend in California. His father was a musician, and rather than play video games at Rick's house, we learned to play the twelve-bar blues. The gift of those lessons and the shape of that chord were both a passport and the invention of flight. Three notes, so simple, the root, the fifth, and the third. With your fingers never changing formation, there are exactly six chords you can play on the white keys of a piano that will satisfy the human ear. The repeating octaves expand that number sevenfold, give or take some roadblocks at the ends of the action. This is how we began. Three notes and six chords in the key of C. I stumbled with such wonder. It felt like God was in the room. Something was changing in the world and in my soul, and just as we were taking flight, the words arrived. I don't know where they came from, but latched to the clumsy progression I coaxed from your body and into that room was a voice, my voice. For the first time our circuit was complete:

Fingers on the keys
Hammers hit the strings
Strings vibrate, creating tone
Soundboard amplifies the vibration
Melody meets words
The unconscious breaks free of its earthly prison

The first sun in weeks came pouring through that wall of a window. Gold paint pulled in uneven brushstrokes across the leaves and branches on the trees outside. Time travel. Confused looks from family passing our little laboratory on the first floor as they climbed and descended the stairs. It was like blacking out and living every second of one hundred years simultaneously. When it was over, there was no light outside to speak of. The coyotes set about their nightly rituals, and I set about mine. Only this time everything was different. Schoolwork, sleep, evening TV. The framework of a day would become an impediment to the discoveries awaiting us in the room where you lived. Our house within a house. It's hard to say with any certainty whether I felt like something was missing prior to that afternoon, but it's easy to recognize, it wasn't until then I felt whole. The fire was lit, and there was something spiritual in its tending. From that day forward, it became our fate: yours and mine, to sort the fire out.

And on the very best days...a song was born.

♫

Chapter 5

Don't Bother Unpacking

I could write about Rose Parades, the crowded public schools, or the kid up the street whose dad designed rides for Disney. I could tell you about the girls and their bangs, hair-sprayed into statues of barreling waves, or about the fourth grade and math drills and how the other kids were smarter, so I quit trying. I could talk about the band I started with Rick Kertes and the talent show where we dressed up like Bon Jovi, or the day he tripped me on the playground, skinning my knees so badly I still have scars. I could tell you about the heat of that first summer and how my father drove me around in it for hours trying to find a shoe store and a pair of Air Jordans. I could say a lot about our year on the West Coast, but honestly, none of it matters much to me anymore. After Stuart died and I discovered the piano, everything else became window dressing. Don't get me wrong, the praise felt good—hushed voices using words like prodigy, and the astonished look on people's faces when I played my songs. All of it filled a well of fleeting self-confidence that I still tend to this very day. But in the end, Pasadena was a flyby.

I could have guessed our time there would be temporary. I had come to believe that our time anywhere was, but less than a year in one place was a new record for my family. I turned nine years old on Flintridge Drive, but my next birthday would find me back in the Midwest. I wouldn't miss the ravine, but I'd miss the coyotes, my cousins and grandparents, and those afternoons at the piano, willing the sun through the trees. But missing things is the price you pay for starting over, and when my father announced that we were relocating to Bexley, Ohio, I was good with it. There was a sadness hanging over our California year, and I think we were all ready to leave it behind. Of course, you can't simply leave your sadness where you found it, but I don't fault my parents for trying.

Chapter 6

THE GHOST
OF
SOUTH ARDMORE

The house at 107 South Ardmore was a three-story, blue-shingled box with a crimson door. The backyard butted up to an alley where my friends and I lit small fires and learned to smoke cigarettes in the seventh grade. Ardmore itself ached for fresh pavement, straining against the root systems of hundred-year-old sycamores and maples. Still, it was a fine street, and a home to countless gardens that bloomed and died like clockwork each year.

If it was my family's brief grieving season in California that drew me to your counsel, it was your little room off the patio in Bexley where I fought to earn it. And while our time in Ohio didn't end well, most of the early days were good ones. You had a room to yourself on the first floor of the house, with two sets of glass-paneled French doors—one set led to the entryway and the other to the front porch, where on her worst nights, my mother chain-smoked Winstons while whispering into a cordless phone. We spent three years there: a small town of

*square, flat blocks where high school football made the evening news
and the American dream was still alive and well.*

♫

I turned ten years old in the summer of 1992. I had grown used to
moving and to life in the suburbs, but this little town felt smaller than
the others I had called home. It didn't bother me. There was something
quaint about a Main Street with a candy store and an ice cream parlor—a town where every kid from kindergarten to the twelfth grade
attended school in a single brick building. Don't get me wrong, this
wasn't some rural backwater, but Bexley moved at a different pace than
the places I'd lived before.

We had chased my father's career into yet another of the fifty states,
and over the next few years, he would be aggressively promoted despite
his increasing loss of touch with reality. We unpacked the boxes and
mapped the new streets, but life in this house would prove different.
Gone were the days of family vacations and my parents dressing up for
cocktail parties. I assumed they had grown tired of making new friends,
and I never thought to question the abrupt ending to their once social
lives. At home now, it was just me and Kate. Emily and Jason were
away at college, and Chapman had long since traded in his books for
a pair of skis and the mountains of Colorado. We would see them all
on holidays, but it was there in Bexley where our once noisy lives grew
quiet.

Walking through the door of my third school in three years, I had
grown tired of being the new kid. I'm sure part of me was afraid of fitting in, but mostly I was afraid of being left behind. And so I began the
fifth grade feeling cornered and lashing out. My teacher, Mrs. Davis,
was animated, well loved, and it's safe to say she was pretty. There
was nothing unkind about her. But looking for someone to blame if I
couldn't make sense of things, I claimed her as an adversary, a plan she
was quick to foil.

It was one of those almost fall days, when the sky gets pink too soon and the weakest leaves are ripped loose early by the wind. I was riding my bike after school when her classroom window opened and Mrs. Davis leaned out, calling my name. I was Andy back then, an abbreviation that took me fourteen years to shake. I rode to her window, aimed a suspicious look skyward but found no enemy there. The way she spoke to me, I felt cared for, and it wasn't long before my levees broke, confessions spilling forth in a torrent of tears: the whiplash of years in motion, the loss of my uncle, and the fear of going friendless. She had sensed the storm gathering in me, offered up her compassion, and in the end, we agreed to start over.

Soon there were friends, football games, and nights sleeping over at other people's houses. I found a sidekick in a kid named Chris Season. He was scrawny, quick-witted, and we shared a love of Billy Joel and black market fireworks. Chris was the kind of kid who built remote-controlled airplanes and knew about the internet before most of the world got online. Like many of my friends that year, we met around the colossal upright piano in the corner of Mrs. Davis's classroom. When she found out I wrote music, she became my champion, insisting I play regularly for the class. Those performances led to friendships and insulated me on the playground, where my lacking athletic abilities would have otherwise left me condemned. Some teachers teach, others save lives—and I will forever be grateful for the kindness of Molly Davis.

Later in the year, I was invited to perform one of my songs at a school assembly. I can still remember the long walk from the safety of my folding chair, past the rows of whispering children with their eyes on me. Taking my seat at the piano bench, I disappeared into the tension that wraps the entertainer and the entertained just before the journey begins—the collision of fear and possibility that one must weather to meet the magic on the other side. I had never known another moment like it, and I felt it wash over me as I summoned my courage and my hands. I placed my fingers on the keys and launched the song with my eyes closed, never once looking out into the crowd. If you're lucky, you lose yourself quickly onstage, the pressure subsides, and you become the pilot of a dream. For those five minutes, the room was mine. The deeper I dove, the louder the cheering became, and by the time I pulled my hands from the action, there were kids standing on chairs throughout the auditorium, my sister Kate among them. I turned to face them, awash in their applause and desperate to make the feeling eternal.

Those days if I wasn't playing music, I was listening to it, and when my ears and untrained fingers finally struggled to break new ground, I approached my mother. By then she had taken a job at the Banana Republic in the mall, and Kate and I were spending our time after school beating the absolute shit out of each other. While I had been turned off by my first round of piano lessons, I was running out of accidental miracles, so my mother helped me enroll in the music conservatory at a local university. Holding myself accountable, I hustled across town on my bike once a week. My teacher, Beatrice Isringhausen, was matronly, strict, and in nearly three years of instruction, I can't recall her laughing once. It's possible she spoke perfect unaffected English, and she may very well have never spent a day abroad, but she lives in my memory with a thick German accent and a look of utter disapproval.

I was a fairly terrible student, but my ear and memory had gotten quite good, and I relied heavily on Mrs. I's demonstrations of my assignments in hopes of mimicking her execution, rather than putting in the hours sight reading. Here was yet another world where a page full of numbers and shapes could reduce me to self-loathing, anxiety, and procrastination. It's a miracle I stuck with it as long as I did. I don't doubt I was a regular source of frustration for her, but cold as she may have been, Mrs. I was alright with me. She taught me theory and fundamentals I would be lost without, and while her other students were required to perform two classical pieces at our quarterly recitals, I'll never forget the night she let me follow the Minuet in G with all nine minutes of "November Rain."

When I think of my father during those years, I imagine a coastline, battered and eroding. He was traveling inward, growing more volatile, and while I've always thought him kind, he could lavish a coldness on my mother to which it was hard to bear witness. His gentleness could turn cruel, and the pendulum on which his moods were fixed swung wide and without warning. When he wasn't working or traveling for business, he stayed close to home, and with each passing year, he spent more time alone, either in his room with the door closed or gone for hours on long drives. It wasn't something I questioned at first—we still went to the movies and restaurants on the weekend, and we had what we needed regardless of the quiet, sometimes uncomfortable mood in the house.

You made a church for me behind your locking doors, and it was there I first believed in a destiny resembling stardom. I wrote songs about the houses and the towns where I'd lived, channeling the voices of my newly acquired idols. I drilled scales and played half-filled recital halls and on school days rode my bike home at lunchtime to feel the weight of your keys beneath my fingers. My prayers from your altar ascended like million-dollar music videos on the countdown for MTV, the same station where one April afternoon, I learned Kurt Cobain had taken his own life. His loss and the sea change it ushered in was felt in every corner of the world. For my family though, there were other changes taking place, and by the spring of 1994, the ground beneath the house on Ardmore had shifted. It would be less than a year before it split wide open, nearly swallowing us whole.

♫

I'm eleven, standing in front of the bathroom mirror with my shirt off, and I'm fat. It's been this way for a while, but most of the "baby fat" kids are thinning out, and it's clear I'm heading in the other direction. This is the first year I'm called names, the year I'll learn that scores can be settled with casual cruelty. I'm not an outcast or a loner, some might even call me popular, but this is the sixth grade, middle school, a time defined by the unfair distribution of hormones. A lottery of voice changes and bad mustaches I have no chance of winning.

There is no more powerful delineator of time than tragedy. Like a great wall you cannot climb, tragedy lies down in the path of a life, reshaping all that was and will be into the "before" and "after." Sometimes the barrier is built brick by brick, a collection of moments followed by a realization that cannot be undone or forgotten. Other times, it's the work of a bomb blast ripping through the center of existence, leaving in its wake a shrapnel mountain. In my case it was both. The wall had been built, but I couldn't see it until the bomb dropped.

It was late one night in the fall of 1993. I had just finished washing up in the bathroom. The moon must have been nearly full, because I traveled by its light spilling through the windows in cold gray pools. Kate had a bedroom of her own across the hall from me, but on that night like so many others, she was crashed out in mine, asleep in the twin bed that had been hers when we shared a room back in Winnetka. So much had changed since then, but Kate still liked knowing there was someone nearby in the dark. Stepping into the hall, I had almost made it back to my room when the voices below, rising in whispered agitation, pulled me off course, steering me to the landing at the top of the stairs. This was an avalanche, a siege. I was standing at the cave's mouth with the tigers outside.

The voices were my mother and father, but the exchange belonged to strangers. This was an interrogation. As the accusations mounted, my mother on offense, my father mumbling his signed confession, the shape of our dilemma came into focus. The landing where I was stationed became a perch on a pole in a gathering wind, and as I listened, breathless, for the better part of an hour, it grew harder to access any memory of solid ground.

Years later, I would hear these days described as the first wave of the modern American opioid epidemic. For my family, it would be our wholesale destruction. The pieces I gathered as I listened to my parents would be a fraction of the whole I would uncover much later, but for nearly a decade, most of my life at that point, my father had been using prescription pain pills to cope with his chronic migraines. Over those years, though he had sought help to break the habit, the habit always won. By the time I was sitting on those stairs, he was so hopelessly hooked that he required a network of doctors all over the country to keep him running. My mother finally sensed the peril we were in, and my father's voice confirmed it. When there was nothing left to hear, I moved slowly through the hall to the bedroom, alive inside a new reality. One where my father, the man who climbed ladders in neatly pressed suits, was a junkie, the scope of his addiction to pain pills so far-reaching that my mother feared his path could lead to joblessness, even incarceration, and poverty. Her fears would soon be confirmed.

Numb, I stepped into the darkness of my room, making my way to Kate, asleep in her childhood bed. I kneeled beside her, gently shaking her awake. Frustrated, she came to, but before she could ask me what I was doing there, I conjured a voice every bit as unadorned as my cousin's on the day he lost his father. I told her everything I had overheard, loading her up with a burden too heavy to shoulder on my own. She told me I was crazy and to go back to bed. And so I did, but there would be no forgetting. For months I carried that secret in silence, and it grew within me like a cancer. I was eleven years old.

In the weeks that followed, the knowledge of my father's disease became my superpower; I saw behind the curtain, but no one saw me. When he nodded off at Thanksgiving dinner, I knew why. When he stood sloth-like looking lost in the glow of the refrigerator lights, I knew why. And when he spent the weekends in his bedroom with the shades drawn or disappeared for hours in the car, I knew why. When I think about the days before I wound up on the landing at the top of those stairs, it's clear to me now, there was a subtle reorganization taking place—lives in the dawn of upheaval. But knowing the truth didn't stop me from trying to keeping it at arm's length. If you've lived in a house with an addict, you know that life goes on despite the horror and the secrets. And for a time, I was able to go on living with my father's disease in the background. Those were still my childhood days of discovery: of toilet-papering houses and burning head-shop incense, of pining for girls I would never dare ask out and singing loud to the radio in the backseat of my brother Jason's car when he came home for Christmas vacation.

It went on like this for months, until finally my father's problem was too big to hide. The inevitable was at hand: his work was aware of his ongoing struggle; they had already supported him through two failed rehabs and were prepared to fund another, this time a monthlong in-patient program, hours away. He would keep his job if he stayed clean. Time would prove he couldn't. When my parents finally sat Kate and me down to tell us what I already knew, it was late in the winter of 1994, nearly six months since the night on the staircase, and the only reaction I could muster was laughter. The secret had become a wound; it had changed me.

Things went downhill from there. Chris and I were still close, but I was starting to spend time with older kids, smoking in basements, shoplifting, and paying visits to the family liquor cabinet. My father was hospitalized for a month, and though I was desperate for him to be better upon return, the specter of his illness, combined with his absence, left me leaning toward rebellion. It wouldn't be long before he was nodding off again and hiding in his room; and knowing his job— and our future—hung in the balance, my mother, Kate, and I began unraveling, each in our own way. Every passing day, another walk down the crumbling mountain. By the time seventh grade began, I was in trouble constantly. In a few short months I had been called into the police station for vandalizing a classmate's house; I had been caught drinking; and my grades were falling apart. Kate was suffering panic attacks, and my mother was growing increasingly disconsolate.

You hope it's in your head, that all the relapse warning signs might have some other explanation, but by then we knew my father's most recent attempt at sobriety was not his first, and it appeared that this one had failed just like the others. He was not without love or wanting. He still held Kate and I and worried like fathers do, and in a way, his tenderness made the scenery of his demise even more difficult to bear. Then one day in December of 1994, Kate called to speak with him at his office, only to find out he had been fired months before. Rather than come clean, he got dressed for work every day and, instead, went to the library or spent his time hunting for prescriptions. After the call, Kate was mortified—she idolized my father, always wanting to believe the best in him, and he had so carelessly set the trap she sprung.

Not knowing what to do, my mom kicked my dad out of the house—and we lived the next few months in a slow-motion free fall. Somewhere in the middle of that descent, my mother insisted that I hold fast to my dreams. I was only a kid, but it didn't matter to her; she wanted to hear my songs in the speakers of her car stereo and made it her mission to help me cut my first demo tape. We found a record producer in the Yellow Pages, and despite the bills stacking up by the window on the kitchen counter, she managed to find the money to pay him. For a while, I think my music was our only source of hope, and those long drives to the recording studio and the time we spent there were like sunlit hours in the eye of a storm. Eventually, the gravity of our situation and my gratitude for her sacrifice forced me to my feet. I gave up on the rebel routine and, in turn, let my mother lean on me. She was carrying the weight for all of us, and Kate and I did what we could to carry some for her. In the end though, none of us were built for the burden we shared.

It's March of 1995, I'm twelve years old, and Kate and I are being sent to California to stay with our aunt for spring break. Something's wrong though; this isn't a vacation, it's my mother's surrender to the gathering clouds in Bexley.

We spent a week with my cousins in the sun and two days in Mexico with my aunt Kristina. I bought a copy of Tom Petty's *Wildflowers* at a gas station before the drive across the border. Lost in those songs, I felt like I could finally breathe again. But when that trip and our spring break were over, Kate and I were confronted with a sudden change in plans. Instead of taking us to the airport, Kristina drove me and my sister to our grandparents' house and sat us down on their living room sofa. You learn, as the child of an addict, the places where you once felt safe have a tendency to spin out of control—and the spinning usually begins with someone sitting you down on a couch to "talk." I have to wonder what that conversation was like for my Nan and Pop. The needle they were forced to thread, projecting strength, knowing our mother, their daughter, was in trouble thousands of miles away. But together, with my aunt, they eased Kate and I into the new basement of our family's poisoned mansion.

My grandparents were sparing with the details, but the essentials cut through: "breakdown," "hospital," and "she just needs a little time." My mother had been alone in our house, spiraling for how many days I couldn't tell you. And in our absence, she indulged the pressure of the monster pressing down. From the edge of that condition—suicidal in the home she made with no one in it—she had sounded the alarm. By the time the news had reached my sister and me, my mother had been checked into a psychiatric hospital, and with my dad in no shape to take care of us, we were stranded.

Days passed, suspended and waiting for news. Then one week later, Kate and I were loaded on an airplane and flown back to a world we didn't recognize. My father had sobered up briefly to receive us, and we visited my mother in a room with gray carpet and blue upholstered chairs as stiff as metal. Promises were made, but my parents had been leveled by a force so big, their words came out like wishes. You could feel the future slipping away in that room.

What followed were like days in a graveyard. My mother came home, her flag at half-staff. I gave up on school, and, guarding the reasons for my surrender, I took fire from my teachers daily. My father moved back home, having promised my mother he was clean, but before long it was clear he was going under. The desperation in his eyes was even more terrifying than the months before. For a time, I blamed my mom for hiding what she knew about his sickness, for not seeing the signs and leaving him before our lives had come undone. But there was no time left for blame or dissension. Without my mother, we were destined to languish in Bexley. So I took to comforting her in the late hours when neither of us could sleep, and our bond grew deeper the worse our situation became.

I still see her in the porchlight glow of our old blue house, exhausted and clinging to hope. A hope that in my eyes fled Ardmore long ago and, without question, would not be returning. I had begun to believe our hope was in California, where we had family who would take us in and where we would be free of the thrashing sadness filling our once happy home. So I built my case, night after night, returning with the evidence collected: scenes of my father's unraveling and a mirror reflecting three faces—my sister's, my mother's, and mine. The hours the two of us spent talking late into the evening left little time for sleep, but it was in those hours, high on her secondhand smoke, where I listened, pleaded, and she finally agreed. In the summer, we would leave my father behind.

I've revisited that sunken city a thousand times, the only thing left for me there is color. The color of the moonlight through my windows on sleepless nights. The color of tobacco burning at the ends of my mother's cigarettes as we coached each other toward the exits, and the color of the dust cloth I draped over your keys as my heart grew too heavy to keep your company. The house at 107 South Ardmore had become a tomb, and my father, the ghost who haunted it.

Leaving him was easy. Whether it was June or July, I couldn't say, but the heat had arrived in landlocked America, and, as always, it traveled on the back of a sweating, invisible beast. By then, I had learned to sleep over at friends' houses when I could, and on my last night, I camped out with Chris in his backyard. Aside from you, he was the only trusted guardian of my family's dark secret and the only friend I still know from those days. Sleepless and aware of the endings at hand, Chris and I abandoned the tent and audited Bexley with her lights out. We traveled the alleys with the moon strung high and diving, but when the dawn arrived, first pale gray, then green, it delivered us back to Ardmore.

The car was running in the driveway. I boarded and bid Chris goodbye. You were already packed away. To this day, we've never traveled together, but it made no difference. You were destined for milder weather, and so was I. For the second time in five years, we wrapped you in blue packing blankets and aimed our arrows west. Only this time you would ride in the truck alone, your passage paid by charity. All the furniture was about to be sold, the patriarch had fallen, and the older kids were grown and living lives outside of this one. We were three now: my sister, my mother, and me. We had a car full of clothes, new music in the tape deck, and not a dollar to our names. But something about it felt like hope to me. And as I waved goodbye to the shell of my father consumed by our crimson door, I realized the power of his parting gift. He had spared you from the pending fire sale and me from another Midwest summer.

♫

Chapter 7

Saltwater, Birthday, and Two Useful Sets of Wheels

The drive was surreal; every mile traveled on the tires of my mother's Camry took us farther from the life we had known. The blurred landscapes of cornfields and power lines exploded in the wake of our speeding vehicle, but all I could see was the repeating, final image of my father, decimated and alone on the front steps of the house where we had left him. Kate told my mother years later she remembered me clinging to him in the doorway. I remember it the other way around. But if I've learned anything about the investigation of a memory, sometimes the facts are less relevant than the scenes we invent to protect ourselves from them.

It was the summer of 1995; I was twelve years old. The weight of what might become of my dad and the growing sense I had been pulled from the water just before drowning were fixed like laundry on opposing ends of a line. Somewhere in the middle was the person I felt myself becoming as our gray, Japanese machine charged a headwind toward the Rockies. No amount of planning or conviction could have prepared me for the waves of panic and breathlessness that met me on that ride, and though similar spells had been common back in Bexley, I had hoped our running might cure them. But running is not a cure; it is an instinct and an action, and in our case, we had been left with no other choice.

So there we were, untethered in every way and hurtling toward the coast, my mother's car a galaxy, a home to three grieving planets. We filled the silence with small talk, with Mary Chapin Carpenter, Tom Petty, and Counting Crows. We laughed as if there weren't a black hole of a man we called dad stranded in a place we called home, where he would end up selling everything but the bed for drugs. I see now the patterns laid bare inside that fuselage, the emerging of a map, the DNA of our family apparatus and its relationship to trauma and communication. In my family, for all the confessing and honesty that takes place in pairs, our walls go up when the numbers grow. To speak truth in rooms of more than two makes it harder to rewrite history, pinning discrepancies on a game of telephone.

You arrived in Southern California before I did. Your very first home near the ocean. The movers unloaded you into a corner of the front room my aunt Kristina had so generously cleared. On the day my fractured family walked, half ashamed, through her front door, it was you I saw first. Your black shell was bouncing light, so unaware of the circumstances. You were the sole symbol of better days, a treasure spared but a stark reminder of how quickly and far we had fallen. The trip was complete, the crime committed, the future I had urged us toward was at hand. My stomach sank.

♫

Our arrival in Huntington Beach was unceremonious. My aunt had agreed to take us in, and we knew the house well from our summer vacations. The cousins who called this place home had, like my older brothers and oldest sister, grown up and moved out. It's hard to imagine the lens through which they viewed our dilemma, but in the case of my older siblings, those years remained a private misery, much of which they were spared.

Aunt Kristina was an eccentric, almost cartoonish woman, with a big laugh, a big temper, and a license plate frame that read "Original Gidget, Protected by Moondoggie." She was built like my mother, top heavy with a mess of blonde hair, bleached out by the sun. A born rebel turned Catholic school teacher, she was rarely seen without a pair of reading glasses fixed to the end of her nose. She lived in a middle-class neighborhood in Huntington, where miles of matching tract homes gathered in blocks behind concrete walls to keep out the sound of the traffic. The interior of her house was decorated like a crafts fair; every surface was a home to wood totems and knickknacks, with not a matching pillow in the place. The arrangement would prove challenging for all of us but especially for the sisters, whose differences would be exposed beneath the spotlight of that shared roof. My mother was practical, Kristina was wild; my mother kept secrets, and Kristina was an unapologetic open letter to the world. The proximity wouldn't break them, but the tensions born of their unfinished business took on the air of an additional houseguest.

And so we decamped into the childhood rooms of other children and unpacked the remains of our past lives. We were in for another hard year. As the days and weeks gathered steam, so did the collection of unspoken house rules, the two most important of which were the preservation of quiet and the recognition of our temporary status there. Kristina had come from hard years of her own, recently divorced and with her kids grown and out of the house; our arrival intruded on her freedom to navigate those changes alone. There would be no more walking around the backyard naked or visits from the surf bum neighbor who had fallen in with a cult. She was doing what was right, but it was clearly an inconvenience, and I couldn't blame her for any lack of grace. For three people traveling so light, the burden of our baggage was, no doubt, on full display, and any illusion of easy company was erased when we first walked through her door.

If you could have spoken, what would you have said? Would you have been angry for my lack of attention and for the dust I let gather on your keys? Or would you have wept at the realization that you, too, were a member of our wounded family?

♫

As with all kids, the beginning of a year is not the first day of January but the first day of school. For all the dread and introspection of that summer, nothing filled me with more unease than the prospect of eighth grade. Over the previous two years I had swelled in size, and while I was no stranger to the sickle of a bullying tongue, the friends I had made before I put the weight on had insulated me from the worst of it. But I had left those friends behind. There would be no cover for me now, and making matters worse, there were no clothes in my closet I could tweak or repurpose in hopes of resembling the herd.

How my mother found the money to take me shopping that summer is a secret she never shared, but the thought of it fills a well of gratitude that has, on occasion, run dry. Addiction is complicated, and there were days then and days still that I felt she left Kate and me unfairly exposed—but for any of her missteps, there was no absence of love and no mother more willing to join her children in the trenches where our fears welled up and our hearts went breaking. She saw my fear and she worried for me, and she begged or borrowed so I might have some new clothes and shoes to start the school year feeling like I might belong.

Stepping onto the campus of Talbert Middle School for the first time that August morning was like paddling out into a subculture tidal wave. The clothes, the language, the music, the methods of transportation; it was the composition of a water wall I was not prepared to meet. And with Kate starting high school a few miles away, I would be fending for myself in a time of little comfort. I had never seen kids like this before, and I found myself judging them while hoping to avoid *their* judgment. This was not the California I had dreamed of in those late-night conversations with my mom on the porch in Bexley, but it was too late to turn back now, and fitting in would be harder than I thought.

The school itself was an inverted world. Devoid of hallways and staircases, the brick one-story building felt like a prison with a palm tree view; a wasteland with year-round good weather, home to diverse populations hellbent on segregation at recess, with class sizes pushing forty. It's clear to me now that my harsh perceptions were filtered through the lens of my family's upheaval, but thinking back on that landscape, I still see it as a concrete canvas with little shade. The abundance of sun and absence of a place to hide I assume proved challenging for Lucas McCreery, one of the few close friends I made that year, whose fair skin and slicked-back white hair doubled as reflectors on bright days.

We met like most loners do, wishing to be otherwise and dreaming of life in other skins and bodies. There's a silent language among new kids and outcasts that is first transmitted in passing glances. Eventually there are cautious greetings and replies, the kicking of friendship tires that, with luck, leads to fewer moments looking over your shoulder at lunchtime. Unlike the conversational English spoken by Talbert students, I understood *this* language and, as a result, spent relatively few days as a cinderblock wallflower.

Lucas lived around the corner from Talbert in a modest house, but despite also being new in town, he seemed comfortable in the clothes and cadence of the school. We were equally decorous and meek, and if I was to guess, it was the comfort of companionship that rendered our bond rather than any true compatibility. I never asked about his troubles, and he never asked about mine. Like most boys our age, conversation was, at best, a swipe at the surface, and I welcomed the lack of inquiry. Lucas's mother, Dotty, was a slight woman with an accent

I couldn't place, but I was too shy to investigate its origins. His stepfather, Beau, was shaped like a refrigerator and always sweating—this accounted for the fans, loudly populating every room in their house, which they left dark to keep out the heat. Beau and Dotty worked for the phone company as information operators and kept odd hours, which left the house unpredictably kinetic or tomblike. I've often wondered what fate they met as the world raced online, but kind as they all were, ours was a transactional friendship, forged in a landscape I would fight to forget.

I turned thirteen at the beginning of September and came home from school that day to find a birthday present with an Ardmore return address waiting for me. Back then, if you were a kid who liked computers, and I was, the new Windows operating system was all the rage. I hadn't bothered asking for it; it would have been cruel to remind my mother how impossible our situation had become. But the shape of the box on the bed and its return address rendered me a knot of confusion. I knew what was inside, but how did my father know I wanted it and where did he get the money? In Ohio I had come face-to-face with the darkness for which my dad sacrificed everything. No threat or loss had been enough to subvert his sickness and return him to us, safely. Yet there he was, ascribing what few dollars he had left, not toward the quieting of his pain but toward the thoughtful quieting of mine. It is *these* glimpses of my father that pressed down like fingers on my healthy skin, locating the wounds beneath, stinging and untreated. Had he simply chosen his addiction over us, it would have been easier to let him go, but the paradox of his love and destruction were at times too much to bear.

I became consumed by the imagined scenery of my father in relationship to the gift he sent me. The search for a credit card he hadn't yet stretched to the limit followed by a drive to the electronics store instead of the pharmacy. Paying the clerk with his hands unsteady, his eyes swollen, and skin splotchy red. Drifting from the cash wrap to the parking lot, easing the car from its space, and lumbering down the road to the post office, the vehicle, a stoned extension of himself. Parking again and pulling the gift from its bag, crossing the lot and climbing the stairs. Joining the queue, paranoid and avoiding eye contact, fumbling to shape a piece of flat cardboard into a proper box. Inserting the software, checking and rechecking the address to make sure he got it right. Sighing with relief as the package changes hands, knowing it will make the journey on time. Returning to the car with the task complete, finally free to focus on the servicing of his all-consuming habit, one that by then required a daily pill count capable of killing an animal three times his size.

Was this the story of that day? I'll never know, but it seemed all too real as I stared down at the package in my hands, which stared back at me, as if bewitched, a home to my father's sunken eyes. Eyes that silently pleaded with me not to forget his love despite his disease.

Since our arrival in Huntington Beach, communication with my father was limited to short phone calls, a shared agony traveling five thousand miles of telephone wire, round-trip. His voice would be thrashed and struggling to make sound, but painful as it was, those calls strengthened my resolve. My love for him had been muddied in the waters of a growing resentment. But, for a moment that day, I let go of my anger, knowing he had not lost all his sight and kindness.

Like my father's gift, my mother's cost more than we could afford, and like his, it eased the burdens born of our unraveling. It was a BMX Interceptor bicycle, just like the ones I had been going on about since returning from my first days of school. Bikes, like clothes, were another way to prove you fit in; coming from Ohio, my old mountain bike was yet another way of proving I didn't. Kate and my mother glowed like a pair of cosmic twins as they wheeled my surprise through the front door. And just like that, I was one step closer to invisible, the greatest gift of all. Perhaps my mother suspected what my father was sending and had hoped to best him with the bike, or maybe it was the freedom of a paycheck bearing her name—she had taken a job managing the Blue Lantern Inn, a small hotel in Dana Point, thirty miles south. But I tend to believe what led her to stretch our means for the sake of that milestone was the part of her that, time and again, insisted on hope in the face of our misfortune. Whatever it was, my parents, both so broke in bank and heart, collectively refused to let my birthday pass without fanfare.

The balloon of good fortune these gestures fixed to the ballast of my family's ordeal provided a secondary gift of lightness, a surfacing above ground I had not felt in many months. I was thirteen and liberated, granted access to worlds of wind and high-speed connection. And while it would be easy to allow the clouds of those years to cast shadows on the sweetness and the laughter, it cannot go without saying, I was loved and there was sun.

After my birthday, there were several quiet weeks at school. Lucas and I rode bikes around his neighborhood when class let out, and with my mom clocking long hours at the hotel, Kate and I were growing comfortable as latchkey kids. My English teacher, Mrs. Frazier, a squat woman with a dark bob and penchant for vulgarity, asked the class to write short stories in the style of Edgar Allan Poe. I loved her class and poured myself into the creation of those bleak parodies. There was a new patio now, where my mother smoked her cigarettes and we confessed our fears, but this time across a table of lit candles in tiny votives. There I would sit, watching the yellow flames dance. And as if scripted by the breeze, a theater of light and shadow played out across my aunt's collection of weird windmills and flags for every occasion.

You were, once again, within earshot, a cracked window away. Were you listening in or had you retreated, desolate and questioning the motives for your relocation? How I had wished to distill the rattlings of my brain upon a bed of your making, but the sound of my own voice was, at that time, a window best left closed.

♪

The metal arm of fall had nearly snapped forward on the turnstile of changing seasons, but the absence of deciduous trees made it hard to tell the difference. By then I had grown comfortable with the workings of a day. I learned the quick routes around town as well as the scenic ones, though I tended toward the latter. I discovered how the Playboy Channel on the downstairs television would reveal itself in snapshots, through arms of occasionally generous static; and outside of the time spent with Lucas and the kids in his neighborhood after school, I was mostly alone and that felt fine. I was diffident and flying under the radar, but the architecture of school life was no longer a source of crushing anxiety, and the concrete of routine was finally setting.

My bike had become a symbol of freedom, a vehicle that allowed me to explore our new planet under my own steam. Then, one late fall morning, I rode that symbol, very publicly, into a spotlight I had worked hard to avoid. It was ten minutes from the first bell, and the car and foot traffic were converging at peak levels at the mouth of the tract that housed the school. I was barreling down the sidewalk when my handlebars made contact with a plank on a wooden fence to my left. Had I hit the brakes then, the scene would not have registered to most, but I was hellbent on recovery and urged the bike forward despite the onslaught of planks jutting out. Lurching, one after another, my rubber handlebars struck every shoddy, poorly seated slat on the fence, drawing the attention of a student body who for months had looked straight through me; but they could see now that I was, in fact, among them. The fence ended, the sidewalk turned, and my handlebars cut hard right, halting the bike's forward momentum. In slow motion, my body was launched over its frame and into a manicured hedge lining the busy street.

By third period the news had spread, and I was "fence boy." A moniker as absurd as it was effective. I lived with the heckling for weeks, hanging my head between classes as the insult rode by on currents of subtle cruelty. Then, one day after English, I snapped at the worst offender. I think Mrs. Frazier had just completed a lesson analyzing Coolio's "Gangsta's Paradise," which, at the time, seemed like a revelation to me. Leaving her classroom, I was rounded on by the kid with nothing more than the worn-out slur and a group of his sloppily dressed friends. Sarcastically, I expressed my appreciation for the clever nickname, took a few shots at his intellect, and threw in a couple of expletives for good measure. My face was, without question, a shade of burgundy worn exclusively by fat kids who have had enough. Caught off guard, the crowd dispersed, and I was left to contemplate whether the momentary satisfaction would be worth the repercussions. Luckily for me though, the episode found a sympathetic audience, including a new friend, Julian.

Julian loved punk and hardcore music and, at roughly a foot taller than most of the eighth grade, wasn't someone people generally fucked with. He was the kind of kid whose textbook covers were canvases for hand-drawn anarchy signs and logos for bands like the Dead Kennedys. He had seen something brave in the confrontation, extended me a hand of friendship, and over a few short days it was as if he built a dam, systematically reversing the tide of my impending ostracism.

Through Julian and his misfit emissaries, I was invited to garage punk shows, where shirtless kids bloodied themselves in the first mosh pits I'd seen outside of MTV. We would shoot skate videos and spend weekends in abandoned lots, crashing our bikes off makeshift dirt ramps. Where Lucas was one of a few true friends, a loner whose company came easy, the expanded circle of skaters and weirdos we met through Julian made life interesting. Those days were a vacation from myself. I assumed an identity out of balance with my nature, but the protection it afforded me was worth the compromise and helped me get through the year. Whatever the distance was between the "real me" and those in the crew to which I had been adopted, it made no difference. I was grateful. And while my days in Huntington Beach are coated with the junk of gloom and instability, that bike and those kids were the gift of an armor and a set of hands on a rope pulling me through.

Chapter 8

Some Flowers Grow from Bone

The call for quiet was only partly to blame for our estrangement. I feared what was stirring below the surface of me, what you might dislodge should I be wrapped in the timelessness of our open channel; this, too, added planks to the barrier between us. Fear has a way of stealing the wheel, but at thirteen, I was too young to understand that. As for the quiet...did you bristle at its breaking? Did you hold grudges against the television and family fights reflected by your echo chamber? And what about the night in November, when the chatter turned to chaos, the chaos into tears, and the tears into a realization: what you run from has a way of catching up with you.

♫

Somewhere between Thanksgiving and Christmas, I was too close to a ringing phone. There are moments in life that age less like memory and more like bad tattoos; neglect them and the ink runs, try to erase them and the scars remain. I have my fair share of tattoos, but that night left me branded.

Kristina kept an office on the first floor just off the kitchen where she ran a side business, printing invitations for weddings and baby showers. I was surveying the pantry sometime before sunset when the call came in. I made my way to the office, past her industrial printer and stacks of blank stationery, and unseating the receiver, I found myself catapulted deeper within the maze of an already lost year. I don't remember what I heard first—if it was him, an operator, or a prerecorded message saying something like, "You have a call from an inmate at such and such correctional facility." Whatever the greeting, it was my father who found me in the static on the other side, his voice ripped to ribbons and shot full of fear as he rushed me off the phone to retrieve my mother.*

Facts were few, but the spaces between them were easy enough to fill in; either the doctors had cut him off or my father's regular supply no longer met the burden of his expanding need. Whatever the reason, having deputized himself the captain of his own stoned destiny, he was arrested outside a pharmacy with a counterfeit prescription. The officers who claimed him had compiled a list of dozens more he had already filled. I could only imagine the sight of him, caught and ashamed. Was he handcuffed in public, thrown into the back of a cop car, and deposited into a crowded holding cell? He went quietly, I'm sure. The hubris of early addiction had long since given way to a shrinking and noiseless defeat.

The rest of that night is a collection of panic-stricken scenes without a thread to connect them, a flip book with most of the pages obscured. A house in crisis, electrified. Tears trading bodies like a virus. Chicken scratch on notepads, and phones pushed to their limit. People filtering in and out of rooms like robot vacuum cleaners, directionless

---

*My father disputes this version of events. Based on his account, I would have received the news of his arrest from a secondary source. (Likely my grandfather.) While I cannot verify either of our accounts, what I've written here is my memory of that night.

and getting caught in the corners. And then there was the arrival of my grandfather. He was angry, understandably protective of his daughter, my mom, but his disdain for the situation and ultimately for my dad struck a nerve of loyalty in me, and I pulled the curtain on my rage. Months of silence were undone in minutes as my anger at everything went ripping through the house like trapped lightning. When it was all too much, I pulled my bike from the garage and pedaled my way through the suburban lamp-lit streets, my tires carving an imaginary SOS into the indistinguishable sprawl.

The image I had constructed of my father behind bars was chasing me now. Was this not the inevitable ending we recused ourselves from? Wasn't this the problem we had washed our hands of fixing? Yet, in that moment, without looking back, my mother was conscripted, once again, to the cause of my father's protection, and in this particular case, his redemption in the eyes of the law. And with her commitment to him renewed, I would be drafted…back to the front lines of a war I no longer believed in.

The night plunged deeper into starless black velvet, but the growing cold and ceaseless pedaling had done my nerves good. I returned my bike to the garage, crept upstairs undetected, and laid my head on the pillow in my borrowed room. The commotion was dying down. Central Time had its toe in the waters of morning, where my father, drug sick in a cell, would wake up shaking with the cavalry on its way. A family friend to post bail and a lawyer who would help him navigate the system. There was little more for the adults to do in their makeshift kitchen war room but ask each other questions for which they already had answers. "What was he thinking?" and "How did it come to this?" And like the heirlooms sold off in our absence, never to be seen again, so, too, became the fate of my seat at the table of "what comes next?" Right or not, my father would be fast-tracked back into our lives. The course was set without consultation or a plan for how my sister and I would process the trauma born of those years. And as I hunted sleep, I was filled with a premonition. If he survived the night, my father would sober up, if for no other reason than to spare himself another penitentiary detox. It might sound cynical, but it seemed to me, there were hoops he was willing to jump through to save himself that he would not jump through to save his family.

If 1995 ended with my father's legal drama, then 1996 began with my aunt trading out one patriotic wall calendar for another and the sensation of being dragged down a highway in reverse. The conversations about surviving as a family of three lay dying at the doors of a field hospital for one: with my mother, its attending physician, and my father the sole patient she would give anything to save. The days were a blur of long-distance phone calls and sanitized news, all with the intent of restoring my dad to his post at the head of our household. It had been hard enough to get my mother to leave him; she had hung on much longer than she should have. While I can't speak to what made it possible for her to tolerate such a lengthy deception, when it came to my father, it seemed there was little she wouldn't risk or endure.

Lawyers had been assigned, and mandatory drug testing and recovery programs would keep the courts at bay. If my father complied, a judge would likely permit him to board a plane and join us in California. According to my dad, he had finally hit bottom, and though my mother feigned skepticism and constructed shoddy guardrails, she was eager to return to a life less like the bad dream in which we had been living. It had barely been six months since we'd left Ohio with little more than our clothes and the car we were driving. I wanted to believe that my father could reform, but the whiplash of this new trajectory conjured incompatible states of mind: the quagmire of a war between hope and dread.

And then there was Kate. I can only imagine what it must have been like for her, fourteen years old, a freshman in a new high school. She always made it look easy, joined clubs, played sports, had friends over within days no matter where we moved. But her trending toward perfection, combined with her chemistry and our family's past, would metastasize into a mental illness in the years to follow. All of which would threaten her life and future.

In the eroding banks of my memory, I try to wrestle free an image of her and me and how we protected each other that year in Huntington Beach, but I am confronted, instead, by two shadows. It's not that we didn't worry for each other, I know we did, but by then we had taken up separate wings in the house of our shared dilemma. The private burial grounds my parents nursed within themselves made it possible for *that* place to exist, and so we lived there like roommates on different schedules.

Grown now, I know what it's like to bury things, and I understand my parents' hope for reconciliation was not in vain, but their hope had a way of prioritizing expedience. Rather than exhume the bodies of their own hard histories, they planted flowers in the graveyard and waited for rain. The rain would fall, and the flowers would grow, but it would always be a cemetery garden. A space more haunted than beautiful, where side by side with our collection of ghosts, my sister and I would come of age.

Time was moving faster. We were sprinting toward decisions. Against the backdrop of family peace talks and the foregone conclusion of my father's reinstatement, I made some plans of my own, boarding school—an art academy in the Idyllwild mountains. How I found the brochure I'll never remember, but in my hands, it was as good as a window seat landing in some problem-free paradise. Eventually, I presented the plan to my mother. She, too, lived in that house without songs, and I have to imagine my absence behind the keys of our family piano played a role in her speedy endorsement. There was no second-guessing or cold water thrown. And with my father still navigating the court system in Ohio, we set about securing my ticket out of the chaos for which there seemed to be no end. I'm sure the thought of my leaving pained her, but my reasoning was sound. And so we filled out the application and financial aid forms, and she adopted my optimism despite its aim to rip me from her fragile keeping.

Were you glad when I returned to you? I wish, back then, I had the words to explain myself. If I had, so many things would be different now. The grief that first led me to your bench, legs dangling, was nothing like the grief that kept me away. The first taught me to sing and the second took aim at the light in me. The contrast between our two West Coast pilgrimages could not have been starker. There is a difference between a fate you choose and a fate that chooses you, between a father and an uncle, addiction and cancer. The growing sense of fleeting control and mistrust of those who retained it led me to pursue a future only your mess of metal and wood could grant. So I wiped down your action with a damp rag to clear the dust and found the box of our old recital pieces and went to work. It felt good to sit at your station once again and fill space with harmony, however out of tune—to hear the sound of our music hanging like prophecies in the rafters. And although this was a colder companionship, I was making my way back to you and to the songs that would lift me from my withering boyhood. And with my foot on your sustain, like a gas pedal in a getaway car, I almost forgot what I was running from.

♫

It seems my life is always waiting for me off some exit at the end of another long drive. We climbed the winding mountain road, my eyes fixed on the desert getting smaller and wrapping itself around the foothills like a skirt on a Christmas tree. My mother was behind the wheel, and the air in the car was thick with anticipation as we landed on the wooded campus. The school was just as I had dreamed. A haven free of culture fiends, a world of weirdos in stage makeup carrying instruments through paths flanked by ancient pines. Was it art I craved or a vacation from my life as a fat kid with an addict for a father? It didn't matter now. My mother and I wandered the grounds silently, waiting for the minute hand to announce my first audition.

When the time came, I shuffled into the rehearsal room where an instructor, a man whose face I've since deleted, tapped the bench of a grand piano that he sat beside in a folding chair. I accepted his invitation, leaving my mother on the other side of a rustic door, where I imagine she wished for a glass to press against it, so she could listen in. The man was easygoing and engaged me in the kinds of conversation prescribed to calm young flaring nerves. Could he sense the saving I climbed those mountains in search of? I'll never know. I did what I could to center myself and played through the selections I had prepared. The first was a classical piece that, upon its completion, I was woefully aware did not meet the school's high standards. Even in my days of study, I lacked a passion for classical music, and at nearly a year without instruction, there would be no convincing otherwise. I could have recited every word of the admissions documents, having read and reread them as if they were a pardon awaiting signature, but my hope had left me blind to my shortcomings. The second piece was one of the last songs I wrote before we left for California. A song about another city I had called home—Chicago, the last place we lived before my uncle passed away. When I think of that song now, it is a memory of life before the messiness of being human, before loss and my parents carrying unmanageable weight. The blue music of desire for the return of simpler days, but desire alone cannot return a thing gone missing. In singing *that* song, I felt the air in the room change and played as if my life hung in the balance. I felt as though it did. If my one-man judge and jury hadn't sensed my desperation prior to that performance, there would be no question of it now. When I finished, the instructor invited my mother back into the room. There was no denying my lack of training, but he had been moved and had sensed the thing alive in me, expressing his to desire to raise it. His candor and affection for my gift reminded me that it *was*, in fact, a gift, and knowing I had prepared a theater audition, he encouraged me to show the next panel of judges what he saw when I played *my* music.

Like my first audition, the school's drama department required the performance of two selections: one classical and one contemporary. Getting ready for the day, I pored through books of monologues and finally settled on two, practicing them for hours every night in my bedroom with the door closed. The first piece was most likely Shakespeare, "once more unto the breach dear friends," and the second was a modern tearjerker, though I couldn't tell you the name of the source material if I tried. The scene wandered through familiar themes of death and loss, and from what I recall, it was written to be delivered from the top of a staircase. How fitting.

The theater was empty but for a small panel of faculty in front of the stage and my mother in a row toward the back. The room was mostly dark, and in the dim stage light I found it easy to step from myself into the character. I knew, in that moment, if I wished to secure a space at the school, this would be my best shot, so I took it. I channeled every ounce of the world I aimed to escape and found myself at the top of an imagined staircase. I watched the words I borrowed tumble down each step, carried across the stage on the tears they conjured. Directions were hurtling toward me from the faculty in the dark, and I executed them as if under some strange power. This was not unlike the feeling of a song being born, and when it was through, I stood shipwrecked and silent before the panel, all of whom appeared equally speechless. Never before and never after have I felt so publicly possessed by another writer's words. It was clear I had done the job.

The sight of my mother as she descended from the aft of the theater tested my levees once more. She had been crying and was struggling to pull herself together. Some window had opened on that stage, and through it, the wreckage of me was clearly on display. I was not an actor. This was not an act. Months of junk strapped to hope in an overture of rising catharsis had left me exposed. The insinuation of talent was just the purging of a buried thing, the desire to be free. Free of my father's disease, free of my awkward adolescence, and free to solicit a fate of my choosing. But as I sat among the faculty in the afterglow, I felt no need to explain. If my little trick doubled for skill, I would accept the prizes. There was excitement and talk of my future. We couldn't afford the tuition on my mom's salary, but they seemed willing to place a finger on the scales. As we drove home through the shifting climates, mountains to desert, desert to sea, the car and its two passengers were floating. Whatever the consequence of my possible departure, this was a victory, a win in a season of brutal defeats. The nerves had cooled, the windows were down, and my mother's pride was on full display as the smoke from her cigarette danced on a highway breeze.

Chapter 9

THE PRODIGAL FATHER

Late winter, 1996. My grandfather George Karl was a stocky but handsome man with a thin wisp of white hair that he wrangled into place with the comb he kept in his back pocket. He wore Ray-Ban sunglasses, ate the same thing for lunch every day, and worshipped the ground on which my grandmother walked. He was a devout Catholic, a Reagan Republican, and drove a new model Thunderbird with the dial fixed to a ranting Rush Limbaugh. My grandmother, Barbara, was as slender as she was vain and as beautiful as she was insensitive. There was a toughness to her born of childhood stints in orphanages and a life filled with loss, but she carried herself with the dignity of a monarch. She worked for the FBI in the 1940s, married my grandfather after the war, and went on to become a print and runway model, a job she continued into her sixties. The weird tapestry of her caring and quickness to criticize made me love her all the more, but it's easy to imagine her as a complicated mother with impossible expectations. Back then, those complexities were lost on me; they were simply Nan and Pop—my tan, well-mannered, effortlessly cool grandparents.

In the family negotiations that led to my father's return, it was my grandparents who agreed to take him in. Under their supervision, he would fulfill the terms of his deal with the courts, submitting to random drug tests and weekly recovery meetings, all with the hope of clearing his name and winning his family back. Outside that, the plan was vague. There was no prescribed timeline for when we might reunite under one roof, but my mother was eager to be out of Kristina's and to move on as a family with my father at the helm.

The house on Seaward Road was beautiful but represented the gradual erosion of my grandparents' wealth. Years prior, they had been forced to sell their home on Lido, an island enclave off the Balboa Peninsula, where they planned to live out their lives surrounded by family. While Stuart's passing delivered a glancing blow to those ambitions, it was the albatross preceding his death that altered their financial fortunes. Before he passed away, my uncle was engaged in a series of protracted legal battles that had forced him to the brink. My grandparents did what most parents would have, giving up everything they could to help him pull through. By the time the dust had settled on the ordeal, Stuart had been diagnosed with terminal cancer, and the future, where his redemption seemed inevitable, was lost along with my grandparents' savings. The tidal wave of misfortune extended in every direction, making ghosts of so many in my family, but none more so than my Nan and Pop. They were resilient and still knew how to laugh, but underneath it was a longing for what should have been, an image fixed in the past where a part of them would live forever. I imagine that the thought of another sick son, albeit a borrowed one, softened them to my father's cause. He, too, had lost it all and was now fighting for his life, so they made the bed and hung towels in the bathroom and opened their door and their hearts.

Every few days my mother, sister, and I would drive south on Pacific Coast Highway to retrieve my dad from his subterranean bedroom on Seaward Road. The memory of those drives is a car of quiet humans and a radio playing "Wonderwall." The four of us would eat dinner at Ruby's Diner or take the ferry to Balboa Island, and when we parted ways, it always struck me how forgiving my Nan and Pop were to offer my father the shelter of their home. I suspect the distance from the scenery of our final months on Ardmore made it possible to believe in his redemption. Time would decide if their faith was misguided, but, in my case, the grace they offered up was contagious. Despite the murky underpinnings of my emotions, I was glad to see my father's eyes so clear again, even if the shame, which forced his head to slope ever so gently downward, made it difficult to hold his gaze.

Eighth grade proceeded on the back of a languid, almost imperceptible crescendo. The return of my father became the destabilizing overlay to an already unpredictable year. School was a known quantity by then, but there were occasional traumas that kept my optimism in check—a brawl between the "white power" kids and Mexicans during gym class; my aunt's neighbor, Billy, pinning me down on the sidewalk in front of his house, dousing me with a garden hose while the neighbors looked on; and a chaotic scene outside first period that ended with me holding a bag of weed, just before the kid who forced it on me got expelled. I carried the stash around for half a day until panicking and flushing it down a toilet in the boys' bathroom. This was the shape of life, and while it was bearable, there were times I felt I was losing myself.

Months had passed since my mother and I had ventured up the mountain for my boarding school auditions, and I had taken to checking the mailbox obsessively for news. So much had transpired since the magic I briefly encountered that day, I had begun to wonder if I'd imagined it. I still visited the brochures like they were itineraries for an upcoming vacation, but the insecurity I had nurtured over several years robbed me of the certainty I'd felt after those wrenching performances. The courtship of my father and his increasing role in our day-to-day lives also served as a distraction from the plans I made in his absence.

Then one spring day an envelope arrived bearing an Idyllwild return address. Like most eighth grade afternoons, I was alone in my aunt's house. My mother was working at the hotel, Kristina was still teaching, and Kate was likely with friends at field hockey or model UN. I tore into the envelope, my anxiety and excitement mingling like opposing ocean swells. Even my lack of self-belief could not rob me of the affirmation spelled out so clearly in the cover letter, which I read again and again: I had been accepted and given a sizable scholarship. My elation was kept in check, knowing I would still need to come up with the difference—no small sum—but it didn't stop me from calling my mother to celebrate. She had nurtured the artist in me, this was proof she'd been right to do so, and we shared in the victory together. But the excitement would soon be shattered. My father, with a loose grip on the reins of sobriety, would make the canceling of this dream his first act of clear-headed parenting in years.

I don't remember where I was, I just remember the sense of pride and optimism being ripped like organs from my body without warning. A confidence so foreign in recent months lay bleeding out in the operating theater of my father's authority, reclaimed. Breathless, I stood before him, barely able to form words. The mass of what he wrought and the hypocrisy of his resolve gathered around a post of rage, splitting my body in two. So cavalier, he slid past my accomplishment as he rounded his soapbox, ascending. No child of his would spend their teens outside his watchful eye—and certainly not at such an expense. I argued with a vigor and tone that accounted for the degradation of his rank in my eyes. In one breath, it felt good to unwind that monster tongue and aim vicious words at him, and, in another, I realized he was here to stay, that he had chosen this fight to confirm it. There would be no conversations after that one. My mother's place in the melee is an artifact lost to time, the ash left behind by a fire. Did we speak? Did I implore her not to turn my future over to the man who'd burned our lives down and let us pack so he could kill himself without witnesses?

I don't remember. What I do recall is arriving at the realization I had been circling well before that bitter standoff, a truth I'd hoped our hard reset would disprove. If my father's addiction was pills packed with synthetic heroin, my mother's addiction was *him*. There could be no harm done that she wouldn't forgive and no shoulder so cold she'd send him packing. The loss of my ticket out was just another casualty of my mother's unwavering love.

Eighth grade ended at a Denny's on Beach Boulevard. Lucas and I sat in a circular booth packed with the friends we made that year, our bikes and skateboards piled high on the sidewalk outside. Most of the names and faces gathered there are lost to me now, but their place at the table I still wear like a badge of honor. I had made something of my wasteland year, even if, at times, I felt unrecognizable. And looking at our mismatched crew, I was filled with the sense I might actually belong somewhere. Maybe not at that school, or even at that table, but maybe in the fabled California in my mind. I had since dispensed of my art school dreams; I don't even recall carrying my anger too far past the threshold of its utility.

Unsurprisingly, my mother was convinced of my father's rehabilitation. He had been sober half a year, landed on his feet with a retail gig, and the extra income made it possible to rent a townhouse in Dana Point where we would be made whole again that summer. I was skeptical, but months of seeing my father with clear eyes made it easier to fall in line with my mother's speedy acquittal. The friends I had made at Talbert Middle School would soon retreat into the static of those days along with countless uncultivated memories. What I didn't take from there, I was content to leave behind.

Just as my mind was shifting from the graduation feast to thoughts of a new school and a house where my hands would be set free on the keys of my piano, I was ripped from my daydream back into the frenzied scene unfolding in the restaurant. Jeremy, a classmate, had exploded into the Denny's like a bad firework. His nose was mangled, and he was going on about a fight that ended with someone's teeth being stomped out on a curb. The more he talked, the clearer it became—he had seen our bikes and was there to hide among us. Whoever had smashed his nose was looking for him, which meant they probably weren't far behind; judging by the looks on the patrons' faces, the cops were on their way as well. Like a rubber ball in tight quarters, Jeremy ricocheted between fear and boastfulness as he shared details of the massacre in which he had just participated. I stared from his broken nose to his shaved head, making contact with the revolting suspicion that this fight—and this kid—were likely tied to the white power movement operating quietly behind the scenes at my school. So much for celebrating. Lucas and I threw our cash down and got on our bikes as fast as we could, never looking back until we had landed safely inside the protection of his neighborhood and its concrete block walls. Ironically, the final bizarre scene in the town my family had run to was me, out of breath—running.

I hadn't yet arrived at the conclusion that the map of a life looks more like a circle than a straight line, but it's not hard to see—I was back where I started. I caged my resentments, suspicions, and fears and got swept up in the trading of one town for the next. I was thirteen years old, and my brief reign as the man of the house was over. I had coached my mom all the way to California, but with my father sober now, I didn't have the confidence to stand in the way of her big plans. If I had, I would have asked her how she could forgive so quickly and forget so fast, but the truth is, I hoped she was right. I had long since converted to the family faith, a religion of new houses and towns where the past was erased and everything was possible once more. And even though I sensed the move was premature, I went quietly hoping for the best. I loved my father and wanted him to win, even if he was impossible to trust. I had lost my say in the big decisions, but rather than grieve, I began the slow process of pulling away.

Less than a year had passed, and we were back in brown paper and boxes. The local piano mover was all you would need this time. Most of what my family owned could be shuttled in a few trips in the back of my mom's new Isuzu Trooper. What my father hadn't sold was pulled from storage and delivered to the little blue townhouse where we would try again. Saying goodbye to the tract homes and all the concrete was easy for me, but for you, who had been stranded in the corner of Kristina's living room, I imagine it was even easier. No more tchotchkes and windmills, no more freeloading and family charity, no more what happens next. In four years, I would be free to do exactly as I pleased, and when I did, I planned on taking you with me.

♫

Chapter 10

JAPANESE SCREENS

I remember every inch of the townhouse on Santa Clara Drive, but it's the skylight I keep coming back to. The whole place would have been a cave if not for the generosity of that hole in the roof. You sat squarely in the shaft of light it generated, which carried sun to both floors of the house by way of a corridor cut vertically through its center. For the first time since fleeing Ohio the previous summer, your presence was not a spotlight on a fallen city but a vehicle for its rebirth.

♫

We had been guests in Kristina's house for less than a year and received this new home with the gratitude of refugees. No failing on its part would have registered with us, in light of the events preceding our arrival there. The years of things falling apart seemed for once pointed toward rebuilding. My mother, sister, and I were no longer muzzled, living rent-free on the kindness of my aunt; my father, several months sober, had rejoined the family beneath the shelter of a shared roof. He had gotten off easy, but my mother's belief in him, combined with her deep-seated fear of being alone, had always been our sail and rudder. As a family, we had chased redemption through five states and more than half a dozen homes, but this time it felt different. From our patio, I could smell the salt air climbing over the cliffs and hear the clanging of boats in their moorings. There was something about the ocean that reminded me of hope.

The house was small, but to my family, it meant everything. There was a bedroom for my parents and another for Kate, and for me, a door-less alcove at the top of the stairs, intended for little more than a desk. I jumped at the challenge of creating a barrier for the room's expansive entry—first with a large curtain, which proved too heavy for the length of cheap metal from which it hung, and then finally with a pair of Japanese screens. None of it mattered to me: the lack of privacy, the cramped quarters, the sounds of the house traveling unabated up to my postage stamp of a room. For the better part of the next two years, my father would be required to submit to regular drug testing, and the absence of his addiction as an existential threat would be a salve, cooling the skin of each passing moment. We had found stable ground in earthquake country.

We chose Dana Point to be closer to the hotel my mother managed, and at only two blocks away, the townhouse delivered on its promise. Understated, in Cape Cod grays and whites, the Blue Lantern Inn stood watch, a humble sentry on the bluff overlooking the harbor below. Like our home, the hotel resided in the town's quaint lantern district, and like our family, its design was East Coast born, transplanted in the heart of Surf City, USA. There were few places with a more commanding view of the California coast and few I've found to be as peaceful. The Blue Lantern was our lifeline; my mother had grown up close to the family responsible for its operation, and when they learned of our hardships, they hired her. A favor she repaid with long hours and healthy returns on their investment. Had it not been for their loyalty and belief in my mother, I doubt we would have gotten back on our feet so quickly.

Eager to earn money of my own, I started working at the hotel as soon as we moved down the street. I carried bags to guest rooms, ran errands, answered phones, and found my hustle and precociousness led to generous tips. I worked hard and loved the feeling of independence that came with a bankroll. My mother was a good boss, and I made it my mission to earn her respect and the trust of her employees. She and I were still close, but our late-night patio talks over the gray ash mountains of her burning cigarettes were becoming a thing of the past. With our free fall suspended, the usefulness of my counsel had run its course. You could sense the quieting of hard years on her, but she, like Kate and I, had been served well by the tonic of morning fog and endless vistas of dark blue water. Looking back, I think we were in shock, but the DNA of shock and peace are so closely aligned it can be hard to know the difference. In the midst of our soft landing, a home near the water and my father finally clean, I latched onto the insinuation that my teens might be free of the toxic drama we had traded everything to escape.

My father's footprints in the landscape of that summer are hard to make out. He was hired and quickly let go from his retail job when they found out about the court case in Ohio. Eventually he went to work selling cars at a local dealership—a job I'm certain he hated but worked hard at nevertheless. In the aftermath of our short battle over boarding school, he treaded lightly with me. When I applied to a private Catholic school for the sheer benefit of a uniform and the anonymity it might provide, he supported me and helped come up with the deposit. And when we attended the orientation and I was so put off by the rules and Catholicism in general, it was he who convinced my mother I should be allowed to back out. Beyond this, my memories of him are of meals at Jack's, the diner our townhouse shared an alley with, and the underlying worry that he could be lost to us again at any moment. I kept my fears to myself. He was my father, he was clean, and regardless of what he had put us through, I was glad to have him back.

When I entered my freshman year at Dana Hills High School, I was an awkward fourteen, powered by fast food and six Cokes a day, overweight with every aligned insecurity. I had attended my fair share of new schools, but the suggestion of a more permanent address put my desire for friendship and acceptance at odds with my usual strategy of skating by undetected. I liked this new place—it felt like home—and I was afraid of botching my assimilation. Growing up fat is a curse no one survives without scars. The heightened state of awareness and constant fear of unsolicited daggers leave so few safe places to hide. The kids at Dana Hills were either disinterested or genuinely less cruel than others I had encountered though, which made it easier to breathe as I traveled the halls those first few weeks. I laid low but looked for opportunities and subtle kindnesses, and slowly found my way to friends.

Adam Trejo was a scrawny kid who was always finding ways to get kicked out of class. He had a neck like an arrowhead and a mouth full of braces, and at least once a week attended school wearing a T-shirt with a cartoon character on the front and a caption that read "how about a nice Hawaiian punch." We met in Spanish class, where our teacher, Mrs. Weiss, insisted on calling Adam by his last name, and the rest of us followed suit. He was combative and kept me constantly laughing, and while he spent most of his time locked outside class, being punished for one offense or another, we became fast friends.

Ryan Daniels was athletic and good-looking, the kind of kid who wore cologne and too much hair gel and was always in the company of girls. We met in drama class, and he, like a good politician, put his arm around me and began introducing me to his friends. Like Trejo, most people referred to Ryan by his last name, and in time, most people referred to me by mine. In the end, I'm pretty sure only half of the people I met in high school even answered to their given names.

As my circle of friends grew—many of them music and theater students—I reconsidered enrolling in the high school's affiliated arts program. After missing out on Idyllwild, I felt like anything else would have been a step down, so I had passed on signing up at the beginning of the year, enrolling in a single drama class instead. In Huntington I had all but quit sitting behind the keys of my piano, at times wondering if music had been nothing more than a passing phase. But connecting with friends between classes in busy corridors filled with theater kids and musicians, I felt my passion reignited, and when auditions for the fall musical were announced, I added my name to the list.

The Porthole Theater at Dana Hills was always hive-like and buzzing, but never more so than it was on audition days. One by one, we would be called before a panel of faculty, and while the people in charge worked to assemble their cast, the auditioning students would be doing threat assessments from fixed folding chairs throughout the theater. I have no recollection of the lines I delivered that afternoon, and the truth is I would have made a laughable leading man, but my musical life craved reanimation, and what came next was a set of jumper cables.

Like a building in a skyline born of puberty phases, I stood shoulder to shoulder with my classmates in a long row on the theater stage. One after another, they stepped forward to sing their songs, and when it was my turn, I did so, wearing my insecurities like a bad blanket. Rounded shoulders, red cheeks, head down. Mr. Woods, the choir director, sat behind his piano, troll-like and irritated, waiting for me to hand over sheet music so he could accompany me like he had the others. Timidly, I approached him, negotiating his temporary leave from behind the keys of the piano, then took his place at the bench. Billy Joel had been my idol since I was ten. His Cleveland tour date in '94 was my first concert and one of the last memories I have of my family together, before my father's disease consumed everything. I wanted those kids to see me like I saw my hero that night, so when I took command of the choir teacher's upright, I launched into "Piano Man." The response was swift—people moving in their chairs, errant cheers lighting up the theater like Sunday sermon amens. As I rounded the novel of verses, I was under new steam, collecting the pieces of myself I had lost in my years of private collapse. It was a scavenger hunt for my soul and acceptance: somehow the two were entwined. To sing and play was to feel whole, to be seen and praised was to belong. The path to myself was my path to the world. In the span of five minutes, I laid the groundwork of identity the same way I had in that auditorium in the fifth grade. I shifted through gears of self-doubt and buried intentions, and then standing before an audience whose applause had drawn me out, I announced myself. This was a future I could lean into.

The first few months of freshman year could not have been more different than my beginnings at Talbert Middle School. I still had a full mouth of metal and a body of unshaped clay, but my early friendships allowed the days to pass with ease. When I wasn't in class or working at the hotel, I was in the theater, hanging out at friends' houses, or writing at my piano. Family was slipping into the background the way it does when you're a teenager, but we still found time to eat together, to laugh and talk about our lives.

There was a feeling of battered gratitude in those days: a tiredness that radiated with the bright light of survival. Simply being there was proof my family had overcome the hardships we faced—and I reveled in the granted wish of our second chance. The house was becoming kinetic again, like it had been when my older siblings still lived with us, and despite fears of my father relapsing, I was comforted knowing that he was passing drug tests and attending meetings in fulfillment of his probation. Kate and I were back at the same school, and the shared halls and car rides renewed the bonds that had languished in our season of private mourning.

The Porthole Theater became the rallying point for me and my closest friends; despite the head of the school's early and apparent irritation with most of us, we participated in his classes and plays. Mr. Rigg, the department head, stood at an imposing height, with a thick gray beard, a bowling ball belly, and a head so free of hair it took on the color of whatever stage light he stood beneath. The Porthole was his domain, and the teachers and students associated with it were intended to pay him respect. My already inborn aversion to authority, amplified by the failings of trusted adults, did not ingratiate me to him, and I bristled at the ring kissing he seemed to silently demand. Furthermore, the friends I had surrounded myself with were cut from a similar cloth. Daniels was living in a packed house under the jurisdiction of Lou, a needling stepfather who enjoyed throwing his weight around along with the occasional insult. Trejo's dad took an almost sadistic pleasure in provoking him and then punishing him for the result. I'm not surprised we found one another or that our circle of misfit gentlemen grew; most of us had strained if not totally broken relationships with the heads of our households. Perhaps Mr. Rigg became an extension of what we perceived as misplaced male authority. Whatever it was, I enjoyed our place in his ecosystem—it gave us an authority of our own. In my case, I took bit parts in the plays but sang songs to the cast in our downtime. I cheered on talented friends and participated in pranks devised to upset the hierarchy. Theater kids are a truly strange lot, and those who are all in subscribe to the drama behind the scenes as much as what's written for the stage. I loved being a part of their world but refused to take it too seriously, and my small crew took pride in fucking with those who did while subverting their king director.

The choir teacher, Mr. Woods, on the other hand, seemed less interested in politics and praise. He, along with a handful of teachers I encountered over the next four years, helped mollify my sweeping distrust of adults. It was Mr. Woods who had relinquished his spot at the piano for my first audition, and though the result was a small part in the chorus, he immediately took an interest in me. Many students regarded him as difficult, and it is fair to say he could be. He had a short fuse and a tendency to scold when disappointed, but he loved teaching music, and I was fortunate to be taken under his wing. It was in his choir room, between classes and after school, where I was introduced to advanced music theory, taught to read chord charts and transcribe my own songs. Throughout my years at Dana Hills, Mr. Woods invited me to sit in with the school band and sing with the choir despite never having enrolled in a single one of his classes. I didn't realize it at the time, but he was giving me the tools I would need to speak the language of music, and, in doing so, he lent more to the pursuit of my passion than any teacher I've encountered since.

This is the backdrop to our reinvention. The thing that had been lying dormant within me was awake now. Your station at the base of those stairs and that vaulted column of light allowed every sound we made to ring clearly through my family's home. It was there, in the little blue townhouse on Santa Clara Drive, where the salt air began to rust your strings, and on days when my touch was too heavy, they snapped and shot like arrows across the room. I lowered your lid and continued the work.

♫

Chapter 11

Drive-thru Saturday Night

By the late fall of 1996, my life was in bloom. I was managing decent grades and slowly emerging from the confines of a protective shell. For the first time in a long time, I felt settled in the world, and at home I wasn't endlessly awaiting bad news. Days were collecting in the wake of my family's drama, and while I knew my father's addiction hadn't simply been a bad dream, the infrequency with which it was discussed made it easy to pretend it was. This was our family brand of "starting over": a rearview mirror spray-painted black, so the scorched earth didn't distract us as we barreled down the road at full speed. If I'm being honest though, I embraced the forward motion. It felt good to feel good again.

People were entering my life now at such a pace it was hard to keep track of them, but it made waking up exciting. Between classes and school plays, friend groups were merging and reforming like a time-lapse of continental migration. Somewhere in that chaos I met Jami. She had a long oval face framed by shoulder-length brown hair, a freckle on her chin, and eyes the color of the horizon on an overcast day. I was sure I'd never seen anyone more beautiful. We met in honors English, a class I felt well suited for until I couldn't get along with the teacher.

Ms. F was a skeletal woman, who dressed up for the job of crushing students, especially boys, and when it became clear I had little chance of making high marks in her class, I turned my attention to Jami. We talked on the phone and hung out in the halls, and slowly our friend groups resembled a Venn diagram with an ever-expanding center. Jami made me laugh, made my pulse quicken, and in a world of teenagers so willing to fall in line, she carried herself in contrast, an original. While I thought of her constantly and clamored to be caught inside the light of her recognition, I kept a lid on my affection, afraid its airing would leave me wounded.

Around the same time, I met Brent and Bodger, the highwater marks of the theater program in which I had become a fringe partic-ipant. Brent was a freshman. He had a broad face and jet-black hair, and his talent was both effortless and impressive. Bodger was a couple of years older than us. He was a gifted comedian and character actor, and though he seemed fearless to me at the time, I think he was as inse-cure as the rest of us, choosing to befriend kids in younger grades for the built-in admiration. He was tall, with a patchy ginger beard, and had two separate but distinct walks—one for when he had somewhere to be, limbs stiff, body leaning victoriously into a headwind, and an-other for when he had nowhere to be, limbs dangling, as if boneless and moving through water. Brent grew up with Trejo and our friendship seemed inevitable, but Bodger's was unexpected. Then one night after the closing of our fall show, Bodger offered me a space in his car for what became a weekly joyride.

I remember receiving the invite and feeling like I had won some sort of lottery. I changed from my stage clothes and waited outside the school with Trejo, Daniels, and Brent, and when Bodger pulled up in an old hatchback, my heart swelled upon entering. Is this what it felt like to belong? Deep at the core of me there was a desperation for acceptance, one that endures on some level to this day. Still, as we set out on our adventure, the night air laced with bonfire smoke, moving faster than the cars we shared the road with, I sensed I was a part of something. What it was I wasn't sure of then, but I know now; it was freedom and the sewing together of separate lives into the bonds of lifelong friendship.

I can still recall the feeling of being jammed into the backseat, heart beating like I'd boarded a roller coaster. Trejo and Daniels sat by the windows on either side of me and Brent sat up front with Bodger, but the hierarchy implied by this arrangement was of little concern. I had never driven anywhere with friends, and the sound of our changing voices blasted by the wind with the windows down moved through me like a long-awaited cure. I laughed at everyone's jokes, but made few, and when debates erupted over where to go next, I stayed quiet and avoided taking sides. As a perpetual new kid, you learn to reveal yourself slowly and move with the current.

There were no spoken rules on these outings, but there were a few clear understandings. Number one, Bodger was in charge. All ideas were entertained, but his was the first and final say. Next, there were two options for music: a local radio station that only played disco, or the tape deck, which played They Might Be Giants. Beyond that, it was simple—drive for hours, pulling pranks along the way, getting as much of it on film as possible. That night we started in the drive-thrus, ordering menu items from rival chains and simulating intercom failure. We continued like this until we got bored, and it was suggested we raise the stakes. Golden Lantern was the main thoroughfare, a four-lane stretch from the Dana Point Harbor through three towns heading east. At the time, it was under heavy construction. Whose idea it was, I can't recall, but soon I was hanging out of the trunk of Bodger's hatchback snatching up every orange cone and road sign I could get my hands on.

Once the tiny car was filled to capacity, we sought to marshal our collection into a convincing scene, rerouting traffic from a busy street into a quiet cul-de-sac. We chose Beacon Hill, an affluent neighborhood in the next town over. With the car parked and the plan mapped out, we poured into the street with surprising efficiency, fashioning the contraband into a detour leading from the main road into a neighborhood with no outlet. Once the display felt believable, we deposited ourselves in the bushes, with Trejo's camcorder at the ready. One by one, cars entered and exited our trap as planned, their drivers, confused, returning in search of new routes, and as they did the bushes awoke, shuddering with laughter. The cocktail of nerves and comradery reminded me of better days in Ohio, when Chris and I would toilet-paper his neighbor's house on the weekends. If only I had known my hardest years would lead to new friends and fast cars, I might not have felt so helpless living through them, but there I was, alive and smiling, making up for the time lost in space.

The stunt had been arranged midway down a sloping hill, and in our haste, we hadn't considered what might happen if someone approached at high speed. We were about to find out. By the time we heard the engine of the charging car, it was too late to do anything about it—and a sense of dread came over each of us as we awaited the inevitable impact. We braced as the unsuspecting Jeep registered the cones too late and skidded into our phony detour, fishtailing, the weight of consequence bearing down on all of us. There was an initial sigh of relief as the car came safely to a stop, but the driver took to the street fuming, and as he ascended the hill cursing and kicking wildly at the cones he had just collided with, he was getting closer to our hiding places with every step. We held our collective breath in terror. For a moment, I thought we were done for, and then out of embarrassment or confusion, a reversal—the driver returned to his car and raced down the remaining stretch of hillside. We paused and waited for Bodger's signal, then scrambled out of the bushes and into the hatchback, leaving behind a mess of cones and toppled road signs.

Back in the car the air was charged with a sense of accomplishment and recognition of disaster avoided. The rest of the night Bodger stuck to a single lane, keeping to the speed limit, clearly shaken by the scene we had just departed. No one ever mentioned it, but you could gauge how close a prank got to crossing the line by how cautiously Bodger drove in the aftermath.

I forget how the night ended, but it was probably at the harbor, smoking swisher sweets and watching the waves batter the jetty. Most of our nights on the road required an informal debriefing. We would talk excitedly, adding layers of detail to the events we had just watched unfold, and by night's end, our adventures would be inflated beyond recognition. The telling of these tales would continue into the following week, and by Friday they were the stuff of legends. And with the bar set high, we'd gather again and drive off in Bodger's hatchback to write another Saturday night of stories worth telling. This became the pattern of passing weeks, and over time, my fear of exclusion was replaced by the comfort of a permanent seat in the car. These outings continued for years until Bodger graduated and we saw less of him and the rest of us got cars of our own. The tradition would carry on, but for me, nothing more wholly symbolized the joys of being young as the five of us riding around in that hatchback with the windows down, laughing loudly over the radio, going nowhere and everywhere at once.

Chapter 12

Young Love,
Let's Get Stoned

We found ourselves convening late into the night, the moonlight climbing through the windows to paint your black body navy blue. This was the land of the infinite. Fertile ground. The distillation of new experiences and emotions riding waves of unregulated hormones. Everything I'd missed was alive again. The way you rocked into the cushion of carpet when I played standing up, the weight of my body against your frame, my foot pressing down carelessly on your pedal box, begging to rip it free of its housing. Sound collected in the ceiling vault, a time capsule with its hands reaching forward and back. Our ritual had become a prayer, the gathering of grateful noise and a thank you to the god in whom I had ceased believing. Still, this was a freedom with strings attached: not those wound with thousands of pounds of pressure inside your wooden case, but those of my remaining years with an unreliable driver at the wheel. So I stepped into the arena of craft, high on teenage discovery, driven by the love of song and thirsting for an independence, both complete and indestructible.

♫

By winter, my infatuation with Jami had become a distraction I could no longer deny—an errant table leg, breaking toes no matter how many times I walked past it in the dark, knowing it was there. I had lived through enough by then to know that this ache was bearable; love and the certainty it would go unrequited. Still, those were wrenching days, all sweating palms and longing, and though I was sure my love belonged to me alone, I knew it would sink me if I didn't confess. So I found Jami after school one day, and we sat on the landing of a staircase, where I managed briefly to overcome my stomach and the churning of its acid waves. I wanted to mean as much to her as she did to me and for her to understand that I had never felt so close to anyone before, but the feeble voice I conjured rendered me inelegant. I stuttered to the finish, a shin-splinted runner, knowing the results well before I collapsed at the line.

Miraculously, my fumbled confession and Jami's polite decline never registered as a failure. Perhaps I had become so familiar with disappointment that I was numb to its effects, but I'm not sure this was the case. For one thing, doing something brave came with its own rewards; I had unburdened myself of the demonstrators gathering in the town square of my heart. Jami heard them, and the humanity of her reply broke my fall with all the clouds and cashmere she could muster. The way she bowed her head as if ashamed she could not meet me in the world my hope envisaged, the angle of her knees pointing toward mine, a signal she wouldn't run. She pulled me from my dream with no request I quit dreaming it, all a masterstroke of a truly magical girl. I walked away feeling alive, injured, but somehow assured our story wouldn't end on that staircase.

Later that night, the reflection I found in the mirror no longer represented my aspirations, which were now fixed to a rising tide. Something clicked. If I wanted to be loved, if I wanted to be seen as I was beginning to see myself, I would need to take control of that reflection and the vessel it served. My life up to then had been shaped by a series of forced transformations. I had been a passenger in someone else's getaway car. It was time to pilot my own reinvention.

There was nothing I could do to stretch my frame skyward, but with discipline I might shrink its footprint. From then on, I quit drinking Coke and gorging myself on junk food. I became a vegetarian and started taking Mr. Butler's gym class seriously. I became obsessed with the dispatching of my excess weight, believing it to be the last vestige of traumatic chapters; by the time spring rolled around, I was closing in on a new form. The growth spurt was slow going, but my braces had come off, and I could fill a trash bag with the clothes that hung like rags now from my abbreviated shape. The experiment was working.

At home, things had settled into a passable rhythm. Most of my time on Santa Clara Drive was spent at the piano unpacking new chord shapes, boiling down radio songs, and invoking an expanding universe of characters and experiences into my writing. Music had become my currency, and I workshopped new material at school whenever I found a free piano and an audience. My weekends were spent working at the hotel, driving around in Bodger's car, and drinking Natural Ice in Trejo's room while playing *007* and listening to Ben Folds Five, Weezer, and NWA.

By the summer of 1997, the hard years felt like history. The sting of trauma had worn off, and the days passing undisturbed felt like weightlessness in a world where gravity was optional. Whether my parents were repaying their debts in the form of minimal oversight or they had just grown lax after raising five children, I was spending my time doing mostly as I pleased. The list of friends with cars was growing, and it was getting easier by the day to pick up and go anywhere. Most of us had signed up for the summer musical, *Little Shop of Horrors*, which at first seemed like a mistake until I realized it was effectively a speed-dating operation with limited supervision. When I wasn't at rehearsals, I spent my time at the beach and Trejo's pool. Jami was still a constant presence, but our friendship had become an island unto itself, one where I no longer registered the compromise.

Somewhere between the smell of sunblock and the sound of the Porthole Theater's industrial air conditioner, that summer lives in flashes of rapid-fire memory: sitting in with the house band before dress rehearsals; spiking neighborhood fountains with dish detergent and watching from Bodger's car as the foam poured into the streets; skimming from household liquor cabinets and pimping beer in the parking lot of the Circle K on Pacific Coast Highway. Every joyful maneuver was made sweeter by the knowledge I had once been a spent thing, tossed about without permission, then laid to rest in the sun. I had come back to life more optimistic than weary, more ready than afraid. I was my own person now, given agency twice over: first by the commutation of my sentence as the son of a hopeless addict, and second as a teenage boy in suburban America, where in contrast to darker days there was virtually nothing standing between me and my dreams.

By the close of the musical, friendships had grown deeper, there was summer to spare, and I was on to my second relationship. Sarah was sweet and stubborn with a slight frame and dirty-blonde hair. We spent a month together teaching each other how to kiss with our tongues. I think I liked it more than she did. Her house was one of our friends' many ordained spaces, and we sprawled out around her pool and yard like a jungle, taking our youth for granted in a climate divined exclusively in our cluster of coastline towns. I had come to live in a state of hyperawareness and moved through those days like a character through scenes in a film, prioritizing a future nostalgia above anything else. We swung in hammocks, laid out on the sand, and for those of us dating, held hands in dark movie theaters. Then one night in July, a small group of us gathered on a beach in the shadow of an abandoned trailer park to smoke pot for the very first time.

It was one of those faultless California evenings. Isaac Aaronson had invited a handful of us over to his house while his parents were out of town. Isaac was a new kid—he had transferred in at the end of the year from somewhere in Tennessee and though his accent provided him with an unfair advantage when it came to meeting girls, we took him in anyway. He was a wild card, the kind of kid who would dangle one-handed from a bridge over traffic to get a reaction. But by then, our weekends were spent hunting cheap thrills and he fit that mission well. Isaac was older than we were and had contacts that lowered the barrier to various forms of experimentation, and that night he enlisted his cousin Brody as our supplier and de facto shaman. Brody had already graduated and he was rougher than the kids we hung around with, but none of that bothered me. We congregated in one of the Aaronson brothers' black-lit bedrooms where Brody settled in, educating us on the tools and the ritual in which we would soon partake. Bodger, Daniels, and Trejo were there, along with two senior girls who flirted generously while making it clear that they were out of our league—a fact I was grateful for, considering the ride I was about to board and its potential effect on my composure. Once the tutorial was complete, we pulled our sweatshirts on and trekked through Isaac's neighborhood to the nearby beach, a decidedly more appropriate location for our departure into the unknown.

The beach was cold that night, and as we got closer, my nerves and the drop in temperature left me noticeably shaking. We assembled on the rocks lining the sand and the bluff's edge while Brody pulled the necessities from his backpack: a pipe, a lighter, and a bag of pungent, brownish green weed. My blood pressure spiked as the device was loaded and the demonstration began. Little did I know, the handmade tinfoil pipe, which had been outfitted with a sink filter to keep the weed chambered, would wallop my throat and lungs with an additional burn exclusive to its primitive construction. Nor was I aware that it might take a few extra chest-splitting pulls to render the desired effect. What I do know is that the others felt it first. I was surrounded by laughter and reverie. I loaded the pipe repeatedly, fearful I would never join my box-car to those of my friends, their collective train now gathering steam on its way out of the station.

Giving up, I accompanied Trejo for a walk to the water, jealous of the discoveries he was attempting to unpack. And that's when it happened.

I felt myself relax, my skin craved contact with the sand. I closed my eyes for a moment or eternity, and when they opened, I was staring into the sky, as if it had, just then, come into existence. Below it, the headlands rose from the earth, cradling the condemned trailer homes like sleeping sentinels. Their once colorful uniforms had faded, washed out in the patina of neglect. Every inch of everything was beauty, comedy, and profoundly more interesting than the short life I had lived prior to that moment. Our moonlit shadows stretched across the sand, reaching through time to pin little red flags of nostalgia to the maps of our unmade memories. The sound of waves hitting rocks and the shoreline, the smell of kelp and ocean water, the fire in my lungs, and the uncontrollable laughter; every sensory detail of that night would forever conjure something untouchable and begging to be reclaimed. This would be the feeling I would seek in many forms from then on; this was the awakening of my blood-born predisposition, a gift from a father to his son.

We broke into the trailer park sometime before dawn, wandering the abandoned streets and homes that blighted the monied coastline. In a few short years, the developers would arrive with their big plans and bulldozers but for a moment that little town was ours. Eventually we ascended the bluff into Isaac's neighborhood, our voices stripped and bodies aching from sleeplessness and laughter. We could have rested at the house but chose to reminisce instead, and when it was time, I walked the mile down Coast Highway to the hotel for my morning shift. The inside of my skull was all cotton candy and the silver-black television static found on channel 3. It was a pleasant kind of fuzz though, and my mother was none the wiser as I hastily tucked in my work shirt upon entering her office to clock in. I would go on to relive the memory of that night for weeks, but I moderated my ambition to re-create it. I can't recall if it was out of fear or deference for the disease that nearly destroyed my family, but early on I was cautious about falling too hard for a fix. Those of us who embarked on that adventure had been let in on a secret, one we would spend the next several years sharing with friends who had yet to be acquainted; but, with a month of summer left and few reliable ways to score, we stuck to our usual routines—driving, listening to music, falling in love, and drinking cheap beer when we could get our hands on it.

With August came the shadow of sadness that trails the summer days of youth. Aware of their rarity, we leaned into the remaining weeks, pulling at the fabric of curfews and daylight. But looming in the periphery was the growing suspicion that I had misplaced my affections toward Sarah. The subconscious can be a terrible thing, and, in her case, I regret mine had been steering me on an unkind errand, because aside from being lovely and guiding me through the innocent wanderings of youth, she was also Jami's best friend. In the end, I would be derided by those closest to us for what they perceived as gamesmanship. If anything, my relationship with Sarah revealed a deficit of self-awareness and features in my programming that operated independently in pursuit of desired outcomes. It would be years before I understood this fatal flaw, but, with my fifteenth birthday waiting in the wings, the establishment of unhealthy patterns was the last thing on my mind.

So the summer edged toward its conclusion, and as it did, I found myself caught up in a betrayal—one that would test a friendship and plunge me into the deep water of my first real love. The impact would act as an accelerator, and in a few short years, the coming of age it brought into being would be charted in a catalog of songs, propelling me and my band into the teenage zeitgeist, a moment I had spent years dreaming of, but one for which I would not be remotely prepared.

Chapter 13

THE ARCHITECT
AND THE ARSONIST

Love is a fucking juggernaut. I was ill prepared and all in. Jami called late one night in August as freshman summer was closing down. I was watching television in the living room, where a large window overlooked the garage and a small footpath to the alley in back. Outside, the sky was shifting through gray and blue changes above my family's townhouse, where I was the last one awake. I had heard her cry before. Her father, Butch, was a builder, and he often worked overseas, and there were nights we spoke when Jami had been overwhelmed by his absence. These tears were different though; they were meant for me, caused by me, and they shook loose the longing I had buried for her. Something had changed; it took hours to piece it all together, but by the morning we knew there was no turning back. I can't recall if this had been my intended outcome, but I would be lying not to acknowledge, that at my worst, I've employed a carelessness disguised as naiveté in pursuit of selfish ends. I had spent the summer kissing Jami's best friend, but one call beneath the dancing lights of a television on mute and that would all be over. This was our secret coronation, a ceremony

Jami and I would keep quiet to add space where none existed—the finishing touch on a pattern I would perfect over time. When the sun rose, we hung up, and I floated through the aquarium dawn, its million particles in the pale light swimming. I had gotten the girl. Sleepless and drunk on the future, the world went dim as the daylight expanded, and I crashed into the dreamless embrace of a hand-me-down couch.

It feels foolish in a way, attaching so much weight to a love that came and went before I could even think to call myself a man. But it was real, and its sunk teeth left marks. It shaped my music and relationships thereafter, and each new height ascended, or depth that plunged me deeper down, begged for words and chords to map the landscape.

Young love is so pathetic and perfect, and depending on the lens with which I revisit mine, I am either horrified by my flailing or nostalgic at the reminder of its purity. Jami and I fell hard, and for months that felt like ages we worshipped each other. The bulk of our relationship spanned a single year, but it would continue in some form well past graduation. She was my person, and I took it for granted, maybe we both did. It's hard to know what really happened for sure.

It was New Year's Eve,
but I was thinking of the summer
knowing that at midnight
You wouldn't be around

The second verse wrote itself while I waited for a ride to the party. I had stayed in all week willing the phone to ring. Eventually, you kept me company, and we made something together. By then, I was working around your hobbled action of notes that wouldn't speak, but the challenge led to priceless accidents. In this case, I'd been pedalling an octave of C with my left hand to avoid your minefield of broken strings, and as I did, I passed through a descending four-chord progression with my right. The piano wire of your upper registers always

*took my abuse much better than thick-wound strings down low. Your
bass clef of thudding nothings. So often in those days I felt like an
explorer boarding the vessel of you, never knowing what discoveries
we might stumble on. That day was like finding an island with everything we would need to survive, the home we had been seeking all
along. And so we unpacked there, vowing never to leave.*

♫

It was the winter of '97, and Jami and her family spent the Christmas
break in Hawaii. We hadn't started fighting yet, not the way we would
in the end, with her mom getting on the phone in tears to referee. I
loved Jami's parents, still do, to this day. Teri and Butch. Butch hated me
at first. He was short but immovable, with wild, curly dark hair and a
mustache. He traveled so often in our first two years of high school that I
was, at times, a more regular fixture in his home than he was—a fact I'm
sure he resented. Over time, I'd wear him down and eventually he'd push
me too far, but the day I stood up to him was the day we became close
for a lifetime. Teri was cool; she drove an old Bronco and was always
working in the garden. She had Jami's delicate hair in a shade of yellow
and treated the weirdness of our youth with a softness and deference that
made me feel both comfortable and loved. While it took years for Butch
and I to make peace, Teri treated me like a son from the beginning. I felt
relaxed in her house in a way I never did in my own, and both she and
Butch would lend stability where my parents fell short.

I passed the winter break pining for Jami, waiting for her call in
a world before cellular phones. This was the most time I had spent at
my house in months. And on one afternoon, the words I pulled from
nowhere into the somewhere of a song likened that house to a detox
ward. The lyric stitched itself to the melody before I understood what
it meant; its mere existence made it true. The best songs simply arrive,
and this one was a cosmic letter. I called it "Airports." It was a song
about love and distance, but it was also about growing up the son of

an addict, and when it was finished, I knew it had changed the way I would approach my songwriting forever. Initially I convinced myself the hardest lines had been channeled from my past, but in the end, I was wrong. A few short months later I would find out my father was using again, the prophecy of his deception set to music. And so I came to understand another fundamental truth—a song can also see into the future. By the time my father's relapse was revealed, I was already on my way. The interrogation of my life and the willingness to name names had become my style, with each finished work a miniature house of worship where I laid some burden down. Trauma shapes you; the rich soil of a wound grows beautiful things. But trauma without reckoning is slow poison. There are days I wish I had known this sooner, but I'm not sure it would have changed a thing.

I think it was spring, but it could have been summer, when the calm of recent years was finally upended. My memory of the day is a blur of rage and retreat. I can't see the room where it was revealed that my dad was hooked again. I don't see my parents' faces or hear their words. All I recall is the shattering of my fragile belief system and the proverbial debris as my father ripped through yet another house with his goddamn wrecking ball. This time was different though. I wasn't alone. For years I had thought of my mother, Kate, and me as a team, a surviving unit, but I've come to realize we were just planets in a relative orbit, our comfort always falling short of healing. This time I had Jami, Trejo, Brent, and Daniels, their families and their houses. I had songs and hope and less than three years to freedom.

I dialed Jami after the house had settled. She knew all of me by then. Every moving truck and breakdown, the years of wealth and poverty, porch talks and cigarette smoke, all the failed rehabs and hours in the mirror wishing I were someone else. I had fit all of it neatly into the frame of my finding her. I had made sense of the journey, found forgiveness for a past I had reimagined as destiny, but this fresh betrayal upset my equilibrium.

Shaping the new reality into words and hearing those words travel the distance from my lips to the receiver, I felt myself losing control. Grief and rage like a cyclone split me from the inside and then tore through my room, transforming it into the reflection of its destroyer. Jami's calm but pleading voice on the other end urged me through the shadow to the other side, but not before I had revisited all my family's twisted history. The reconciliation had failed, the patriarch had fallen for good, taking with him the mother whose misplaced faith in him had been my lodestar for too long. I dragged Jami with me into the darkness, and she led me out. An exorcism took place there. The dispatching of a violent and unpredictable weather system. My trust had been broken. I was changed.

By the time the phone was resting in its cradle and my wrung-out body found the mattress and some sleep, I had grieved the loss of my parents. I would learn to live among them expecting little and asking for less. I would be happy in spite of them. My father would go to rehab again and for decades would insinuate his sobriety despite warning signs to the contrary. My mother would cover for him with the tacit endorsement of a blind eye and turned head. I learned young I couldn't trust my dad, but I came to view my mother as his accomplice, believing she had chosen him over my sister and me. Maybe it wasn't fair, but I struggled to see it any other way. I got comfortable with the assumption my father was still using and erected a boundary through which neither of my parents would be allowed to pass with ease. They would continue to be loving and supportive despite their failings; we would celebrate life's victories and mourn its losses together, never discussing the addiction or the years it stole from us. My father would cycle through a long list of careers and startups, some lasting a few years, others ending as quickly as they began, but he would never be arrested again or sell our things for drugs. For a long time that was enough for me. Maybe he was clean, maybe he wasn't, but I couldn't be a cop and a kid, and by the time I was out of the house, I couldn't be bothered. My parents made their pact; I chose myself over their shared disease.

In my sister's case, it wouldn't be so easy. Kate would struggle with panic attacks and depression throughout her remaining high school years, only to find those struggles exacerbated by her transition into college. And while it's not my story to tell, what I will say is that her journey, one born of chemistry and its collision with our past, was likely more harrowing than anything I'll write about here. I know more about it now than I did then, or perhaps I was too focused on my own dreams to realize hers were being blown to pieces. But when my parents were called on, they did for Kate what I was unable to do: be there for her and walk her through a seemingly impenetrable darkness.

I had made my choice and didn't look back, not until the dark flowers of my youth had sprung up in me. The instinct to run, the selective memory, and vice with its gravitational pull. By then I was testing the boundaries of love and distance on a new girl and captaining my own chemical explorations. Eventually, I would build something from nothing with my music, and people would call it success, but in the end, I would blow it all up just to see where the pieces fell. I thought I was an architect. I was an arsonist.

It was the summer before my junior year, when I left you alone by yet another window in another blue house. The landlord had sold my family's little place on Santa Clara Drive, forcing us to leave behind the room where you and I found "Airports" and the fire I thought had been lost to darker years. I had friends to make music with now, and I did what you do when you're a kid in a band: I moved into the garage and played loud. You heard all of it I'm sure, and I have to wonder if you felt deserted or if you understood there wasn't any other way. You were limping, running out of strings and playable keys, and even if you weren't, it's likely that you would have drowned beneath the waves of amplified guitars. So you heard me and my four friends learning the songs that would deliver me the dream we first dreamed together. High school would come and go, and soon after I'd be gone, too, only coming back for that brutal September when I doubt you recognized me anyway. Eventually, I would come into some money, and out of guilt and love for what we made together I'd gift you a new set of strings and a proper once over. My mother promised to play you again, but she rarely did. Years later, I'd find out in passing, my parents planned to sell you before they left Southern California for good—they wouldn't have room for you where they were going and they could use the money, they said. After years of making peace with the history you helped me navigate, for the first time since my father's relapse, I would feel betrayed. I lobbied to keep you in the family, and they eventually agreed, signing you over to me, once and for all. A birthday present. I didn't have a place for you either, but I had a plan. You live now with a friend; he has a child not much older than I was when we first met, and she plays you every day, like you deserve.

♫

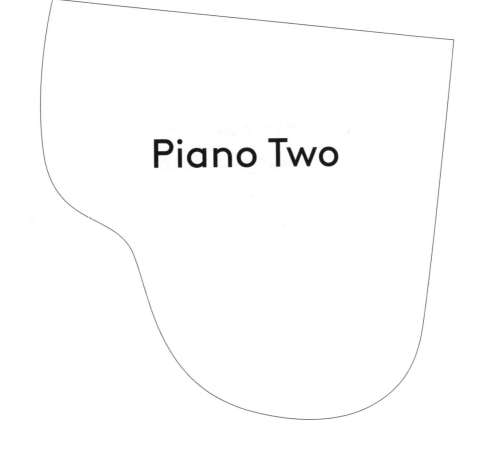

Piano Two

The Less Than Humble Upright Falls

More than one hundred years passed
before Cristofori's invention was reliably revised
into what we now call the upright piano.
Makers from Italy to Austria and the United
States were credited with early models, flipping
the soundboard, brass plate, and strings
on their side, making the upright more accessible
by way of its compact nature. But it wasn't
until 1826, when the mechanical action was
invented, that the upright became as playable

as its predecessor. It is fair to say that the grand

piano, when built well, is more sought

after for its tone and aesthetic, but the upright,

with its ingenious action, loaded with springs,

which send its horizontal hammers home to rest,

is arguably the more impressive design.

For it is gravity and the ability to defy it that

conjures the imagination in ways other inventions

never will. And with its body like a skyscraper

and its insides working against the laws

of nature, the humble upright piano is every

bit as elegant as the grand.

Chapter 14

Slingshots at Dawn

We met somewhere outside Boise in the summer of '02. You were the gift of a sponsor. Japanese black satin, just like my first piano, only you stood upright and tall. I never learned to play like the greats I briefly studied, or the modern masters for whom such a gift would be well deserved. Great playing moves me, but it's always taken a back-seat to words, melody, and form: the towering structures of heart-breaking songs. Still, you were my first true weapon...and there we were, meeting behind a pop-up stage in a parking lot in the middle of some American teenage hellscape. To say I remember it perfectly would be a lie. No doubt, the trapped heat from the summer sun was rising off the asphalt and the air was thick with the dirt kicked loose in the circle pits. There was no ceremony or time to reflect, just a rushed huddle behind the stage where my band's gear had been scat-tered by our amateur road crew: high school friends we had employed loosely since the van days. The music coming from the stage postponed our proper introduction, but I took a moment to pull my hands across your action and get a sense of you. Something was wrong. Our first conversation would be about injury and repair—a sign of things to come. There were chips in your lacquer, scratches on your soundboard, and stuck keys with pieces of rock wedged between them. None of it made sense. You were so new; how could you already be so broken? In the chaos of wrangling the gear, I tended to your wounds while the crew worked hard to avoid me. It wasn't until we had finished our set that the cause of your condition was revealed. The forklift assigned to transport you from the tour bus to the stage had encountered rough terrain on its long journey. The crew had watched as your unstrapped body was launched from the arms of that wicked machine, and in a combination of haste and fear of reprimand, they attempted to hide any signs of the disturbance. You were tough though, unfazed, and thus began a partnership forged in loud spaces where anything could go wrong and often did. Bad soundman after bad soundman strapped garbage pickups to your wooden beating heart, and no one seemed to care or know the difference. I did, but those days were about viscera; precision would come later. I burdened your brand-new skin with stickers from shitty punk bands out of self-consciousness and sheer boredom. Those plastic tattoos collected on your casing even more rapidly than the ink did on my arms. You gave me an air of legitimacy in a world I couldn't understand. Three-chord punk, screamo, emo, ska, hardcore, post hardcore, rap rock, nu metal, what the fuck was any of it? What were we? Kids with dreams, faking it on stages for other kids with dreams. We weathered a thousand sweat-filled dance halls and dirt racetracks before I retired you to a bedroom in the house you helped me build, and there, we built something together... the love letter to youth and abandon we would finish just in time.

Don't tell the others, but you were always my favorite.

♫

No one prepares you for your dreams coming true. It turns out no one prepares you for much. We called ourselves Something Corporate, and by the time we reached Boise that June, we had been a band for nearly four years, a fact that did little to belie the perception of our overnight success. I get it. I was nineteen and signed a record deal less than a year after my high school graduation. As far as the world was concerned, one day I didn't exist and the next I did. But what I can assure you about the years preceding the slingshot ride my band and I were about to embark on is that we clawed our way from my parents' garage through a maze of trap doors and shady characters to get there.

We were five in all. Josh, the bleeding-heart guitarist and my second in command. He and I were alike; having grown up heavy, we spent our adolescence fighting with the mirror. We had forged a friendship in the autumn of my junior year of high school, Josh hunched over the knotty wood of his Martin acoustic and me at the piano in another of my family's rented homes. This one had yellow interior walls and a pale blue carpet bruising in three places beneath the weight of my first piano. What Josh and I found there—without knowing we were searching—was the gift of flint and rock, and the spark that led to everything.

Our drummer, Brian, was a rail-thin surfer, fair skinned, freckled, and stubborn as a drunk at last call. He grew up in his father's music store, where he learned the secrets of rhythm and song. To this day, I've met few who carry those secrets more deeply in their bones than he did. Easily distracted and rarely on time, Brian was always returning from some misadventure with a story to tell. He was someone you wanted to know; when he laughed you laughed, and, in the end, when our patience for each other would be stretched to the point of breaking, we would still find a way to stay friends.

William played the guitar and sang harmony and was as self-conscious as he was good looking, a combination that made him more charming than vain. In the early days we were close. Will was a talented singer-songwriter with ambitions for stardom that mirrored my own. I think it's fair to say that the shelving of those ambitions haunted him at times, making it difficult to find satisfaction in the background. I wish that I had had compassion for him then, for the dream he sacrificed to join us, but toward the end I would carry a quiet contempt for what I perceived as his lack of commitment.

Kevin played bass, but we called him Clutch, and he hid beneath a brown shag haircut and a pair of aviator shades. We had known each other since my freshman year when he'd been a regular in Bodger's car on our weekend joyrides. Kevin grew up with less, and it made him both tough and reliable. Even after the band got big, it wasn't uncommon to find him in the trailer with the road crew, packing gear at the end of the night. Like me, Kevin grew quiet over time, and I suspect there were parallels in our past that informed his retreat in the face of our increasing dysfunction.

The band had been mine in high school; they played my songs and followed my lead from cafeteria stages to our early days in the clubs, but it belonged to all of us now—and the bullet we were strapped to would soon rip through blue sky and heaven. The only thing left to do was hang on.

Chapter 15

TENAGE
ROCK STAR

*Prior to our shotgun wedding, I shared my secrets with lesser machines.
It's important you know this, because it is those secrets, written on
mistress keys, which became the songs we first played for the world. I
was sixteen when I abandoned your predecessor for a keyboard in the
garage that, by then, had become my second home. A world of switched-
off instruments, switched on for weekly band practices. I worked there
without distraction among the boxes of orphaned yearbooks and useless
winter coats, writing songs about love and car crashes, kissing drunk
girls and chasing moving trucks down American highways.*

*In the band's first year together, we played churches, school lunch
hours, and garage shows for friends. Then in the fall of '99, the owner
of a local club called the Coach House took a chance on us and changed
everything. His name was Gary, he was a stout man, always dressed
in denim with stringy shoulder-length white hair, a potbelly, and a
voice like a buzz saw. From the very first night we played his club, he
wrapped his arms around the band and made a mission of our success. I
was seventeen and found my faith on his stage, born again beneath the
cheap lights and the racket. The crowd packed into the club's vermilion*

booths and banquet tables, their shadows framed by wood accents and lights kept dim to hide what needed hiding. They liked what they heard, so I started skipping school and calling newspapers hoping they would tell our story, a high school band with no record deal, packing clubs from Orange County to Los Angeles. Jami and I had become something of a cliché by then, our relationship a carousel in constant motion, but she taught me about love, how it can consume you, and how there are some things you can't take back. And on the day I graduated high school, I sat with the friends I met in the wake of my family's dilemma, waiting for my name to be called and for life to begin.

It did.

Gary, our denim-clad benefactor, had paid for the band to make an album, and I recorded my parts on his club's concert grand. With school behind me and the crowds getting bigger, it wasn't long before word reached the kingmakers in Los Angeles. Then in the spring of my eighteenth year, with the garage door sky-high, we played a concert for the neighborhood and the sibling owners of an indie label called Drive-Thru Records. They offered us a deal on the spot. There were contracts, lawyers, agents, showcases, a studio piano with a buzzing bass string, and an old upright I tattooed with a Sharpie marker, commemorating every date and stage we played together. There was the van we called Morrison and the trailer we called James, home to my band's gear and bodies as we explored America one dive after the next. And then there was you.

For years before we met it was like this: a cascade of conquering days with nothing but my guts for steering. I had quit wandering history's halls, asking questions about trust and healing. I was done with all that, engaged in the pursuit I had dreamed of when I latched myself at nine years old to my first thousand-pound balloon. I had to do the first part without you. I'm glad I didn't know what I was missing.

♬

Chapter 16

Teeth Cutters in the Parking Lot

Being nineteen and cut loose in the world is a miraculous frame for existence—floor sleeping and broke, binge drinking and then waking up in bathtubs with dried puke on your clothes. Only through the lens of a thing set free, prior to the sunk teeth of luxury and winning, could such bleak rites of passage wind up in the category of crave-able nostalgia. But that was life on the road. We were kids, clocking highway miles in pursuit of an impractical dream, but the farther we traveled, the more clear it became, our dream was coming true. It was June of '02, I was a teenager on a tour bus, doing what I loved, and loving every minute of it.

The Warped Tour has been referred to, by many, as a punk rock summer camp and, by others, as an exercise in deprivation and misery. For my band it was our launchpad. Imagine Coachella, then substitute the fake grass with asphalt and the MDMA with cheap beer—if you're even old enough to drink with the pissed-off parents riding out their day in the concourse. There were no dressing rooms or private showers, no rider with snacks and good booze to help you pass the day. You rose early to hunt for your case of beer and water. You sweated with the fans and slung your own merch, and at night when the crowds cleared out, the backstage lot came to life with the exhausted souls just finishing their circus workday.

Something Corporate was signed young and sent out on the road, where we had been living for more than a year. Drive-Thru, the record company whose owners discovered us, was an independent with cachet, but the band and I had our hearts set on a major label, so they partnered with MCA for our deal. The benefits were huge. We had the support of the Drive-Thru staff and fans, with the album and marketing budgets of a major. As a kid, I was recording down the hall from Tom Petty and the Heartbreakers in a studio the Beach Boys had once called home. We made music with giants like Paul Buckmaster, whose string arrangements appeared on albums by David Bowie and Elton John, and we were being flown around the world to play showcases and shake hands. If every moment were a scene in a movie, then what came next was a frenzied montage of crowds, the grind, and our eventual success. We were worming our way through the teenage underground, with a new record and a minor hit about a high school bully, which is how we ended up on the Warped Tour with a hundred other bands and a bus driver named Harley.

In the beginning, our sets were a ghost town, but even the spottiest crowds were home to hecklers with their middle fingers raised high overhead in opposition. I was a piano player, a singer-songwriter, and as a band we were, without question, the most unpunk thing at the punk show. The Doc Martens set, with their mohawks and earlobes stretched to their shoulders, had designs on making us pay, but their hatred galvanized us, and for thirty minutes a day we went to war under the blistering sun. Some days it rained bottles and shoes, other days it was dirt, rocks, and spit. And on one particularly confrontational afternoon, I took a full block of ice to the face on a stage somewhere in the middle of Texas. But we didn't give up, and I bled for my songs alongside my brothers until the crowds turned in our favor.

We were cutting our teeth, learning how nerves corrupt tempo and guitars need constant tuning, and how diving off a speaker stack into a crowd could kill you, but it might also make you a hero. We had been playing shows for years, but the boot camp nature of those summer days and the tutelage of seasoned bands and road crews gave us something toward which to aspire. We got better each week, and as we grew, the crowds grew with us. By the end of the tour, my view from center stage was one of apocalyptic beauty: wrung-out bodies, dirt kissed and pressed against the barricades; crowd surfers on their violent journeys; paradoxical mosh pits springing up like clear sky hurricanes, and my favorite sight of all...the jumping—endless and in unison as if the earth before our inconsequential everything had been wired to a current and triggered by the kick.

I started dating Kelly the previous summer, and by then she was used to the lifestyle. We would pick her up at the airport in the tour bus, and she would ride with us for days before flying back to school, the two of us sleeping in a bunk no bigger than a coffin. It was a strange way to be in love, but we saw the world together without stepping foot in a hostel, and I can't say I'm mad about that. We had known each other since I was fifteen, when she began hanging out with my sister Kate. Kelly was beautiful even then, with eyes of jade and hazel and a dimple on both banks where the river of her smile ended. In high school, most of Kate's friends were swept up in a youth group movement that found many of them, my sister and Kelly included, born again beneath a neon cross. I found their faith alarming. I had walked out on Jesus in catechism class and was deeply suspicious of people who believed in miracles. But that was high school, and by the summer of '01 we were different people.

Kelly had come home from college with the rest of the prodigal alumni to vacation among the holdouts and drifters—waitstaff, bartenders, video store clerks, and valet parkers who had made peace with their lack of ambition. Those were my people, and I spent my year after graduation working on the band and partying with them. I had fallen for Kelly the previous summer at a party that ended with us sitting too close on the tailgate of a moving truck, but there was no sense in our connection yet. I spent the intervening year never sleeping, booking shows, and writing songs while she was shaking off her faith on dance floors in Italian discos. We flirted in digital threads beneath mass emails about her term abroad in Florence, my upcoming gigs, and the where-abouts of our wandering friends, and by the time she arrived back in town, we had evolved in each other's directions.

She was just as I remembered, but more complex, expanding like colored ink on gauze. She was coy, questioning and prepping her rebel-lion against a world that had discounted her as demure, devout, and soft to the touch. By then I had found my nerve for most things; I was self-possessed to the point of arrogance, and while it gave me an edge elsewhere, it took months to bring Kelly around.

There were bonfires and a night swim where we floated through the dark: magnets in water and magnets in the open air. There were punk rock shows in strip malls, fake IDs, and a table at the Trocadero on Sunset Boulevard where I wrote down every word. There were parties at the band house and a staircase first kiss—Kelly was in boxers, and we talked until dawn. Then there were dry socket wisdom teeth and the Christian missionary pen pal, whose return home threatened to put an end to it all. And when it appeared that my plans for us might not work out, I wrote a song about the nights I thought they would, and I played it everywhere I went, hoping she'd hear it and change her mind. Finding her had been like finding the piano on Flintridge. Before the music, I didn't know what I was missing, but once I heard it, I was never the same. Kelly was like that music, so I refused to give up, and slowly she began to see what I saw in us. It was a gamble; she was already family, one of Kate's closest friends. I would be leaving for tour soon, and she would be off to school, and while so much about a life together made no sense, it felt impossible to live any other way. Eventually, in a harbor bar, while a lounge singer did his best Elvis, I made my intentions clear—wherever I was going I was taking her with me. She agreed, and we never looked back.

From then on, the scenery shifted around us, sometimes by the hour, our story unfolding against a tapestry of cities, stages, and truck stop days off. Our world was simple then. We had each other, she had school, and I had the band. The containers of our separate lives were no match for what we shared, and despite our seemingly opposed pursuits, Kelly was the gift of earth for me, and for her I was the gift of sky.

With the tour ending, she was gearing up for her last year of college, and I was wrapping up my studies on the impact of gravity bong hits and shotgunned beers in parking lots beneath clouds of trapped diesel. The band returned home before the end of August, but by then the concept of home had been amended and ratified. Home was a mailbox and a mattress between tours, which were stacking up like cars in holiday traffic. It was nearly autumn, two thousand and two, and I was about to turn twenty years old.

You rode in a baby blue case, strapped to the trailer's wall just over the front tires near the locking ball hitch. Feet from you and your shell within a shell, I would get lost within the engine's drone lullaby. Some nights I counted mile markers from the windows of the bus's back lounge, others I crashed party-sick in the catacombs. You were my workhorse onstage and my palm reader everywhere else, and some nights when the show loaded out, the crew packed you last so we could tend to the fire by moonlight. You were already everything, but in time you'd be more: a mirror, a projector, a place to rest my hands and head, too young to be so weary.

♫

Chapter 17

Tin Cans, Tires, and Wings

Glasgow, Munich, London, Bologna, Amsterdam, Sheffield, Berlin... I had never left North America, and suddenly my passport resembled a doormat. We had a European tour manager named Carlos, a giant sweating man who insisted on three showers a day. He was rough on the road crew, held the band's shared cell phone hostage, and we had to threaten to fire him more than once for refusing to let us call home. I smoked hash in Manchester, walked the Reeperbahn in Hamburg at midnight, and the band and I got stoned offstage by a crowd of angry Italian metal heads in Bologna. We were an international band now, waking up in a new country every morning and getting paid for it. The label showered us in expensive gifts, footing the bill for decent hotel rooms on press days, and when it was over, we flew back to the States and played fifty more shows before Christmas.

We had been adopted by our label mates, a punk act called New Found Glory, who, during our nearly four months touring together, were finding success in the mainstream. Watching your friends get famous is a trip. It happens fast, and in most cases, they're too busy to enjoy it, but, as a spectator, it's no less awe inspiring than a shuttle launch.

Our shows together were ritual chaos. In those days, you'd throw four bands on a bill and charge twenty dollars for a ticket. As a support act, you'd be lucky to have ten minutes to get on and off stage between sets; the rush from trying not to piss off the headliner's crew could be as thrilling as the show itself. Like the Warped Tour, we were a novelty on the bill, outsiders in a world of outsiders, but no one seemed to care. Night after night, we played to thousands of kids losing their minds from curtain to curtain. We became close with the bands on the tour, the way you do on the road when you're young—knocking on bus and dressing room doors looking for trouble and a little company. The main support act was a band called Finch. They had signed to Drive-Thru around the same time we did, and we had been playing on the same bills for months. If *our* stage show was a party scene from a teen movie, *theirs* was a coven, replete with strobe lights and blood-curdling screams. But no matter how different our music was, we were like family, lending shoulders when needed, cheering from the stage wings, and enabling each other's vices when the work was finished and sometimes when it wasn't. As a member of a warm-up act with a short set and hours to kill, I was free to nurture my growing fascination with pot and alcohol, though I'll admit it was the pot I preferred. I was young and fucked up, being carried through the world on a ticket written by my voice and hands, and it was, in a word...sublime.

Not everything was perfect though. With a closer view of the machinery powering our friends' success, it became clear our manager wasn't up to the task. For years he'd been our hype man, the kind of guy who wore sunglasses inside and oversized Lakers jerseys to business meetings. And though we loved him, we had outgrown him. I was getting phone calls every day about botched business and missed opportunities; panicked over the potential fallout, the band and I decided to let him go midtour. We tried letting him down easy at first, but our compassion wore thin when he refused to release us from our deal, going on to collect money for years of work he would never do. Some contracts are like paper ghosts and his haunted me well into my twenties, but I signed it, so that's on me.

Bad deals aside, we were selling records, and the months of high-profile opening dates had cemented Something Corporate as a legitimate touring band. We brought on new managers, with big acts and platinum albums on their office walls, and with '02 winding down we set our sights on a headlining tour of our own. We would have little more than a month at home around the holidays to prepare, a moment I chose to pack my things and relocate to Murrieta, California, a desert town of cheaply built houses, big box stores, and chain restaurants, roughly an hour inland from the coast and the towns I had called home. By then my brief visits back were underscored by my parents' lengthy interrogations, and something about their fascination with my life and business triggered my defenses. I don't blame them for it, but my inability to reconcile our past made it difficult for me to share with them what I was building in spite of it. It seemed to me they were seeking an absolution granted by time and my good fortune, but the more I attained and the farther I traveled from the smoldering city of my youth, the less I wished to be reminded of it. So, when Jordan, New Found Glory's singer, offered up the guest room in his newly built home, I quickly agreed to move in.

You met me in that wasteland village, where I paid the movers to haul you upstairs so we could convene for the first time in a space of our own. I bought a BMW and smoked weed all day, hunting for new songs while construction crews rushed to build a city with a bull's-eye on its back. America was getting fat and racing toward war, while I got high and waited for Kelly to finish class. She would pull up around sunset; we'd drive my status symbol to the Dairy Queen and kill Blizzards in my bedroom beneath the glow of a 40-watt blue bulb. The break only lasted a month, maybe two, but those days were my first taste of solitude and choosing, and I chose you. You and the girl with the green eyes.

♫

The time on my own served me well, and the freedom from watchful eyes made each day feel criminal in its simplicity. If I chose to sleep in or not sleep at all, if I spent the morning stoned playing the same three chords or just spent the morning stoned, there was no one there to intercept my drifting. It would be years before Kelly's worry for my love of altered states would attach itself to a concern shaped like conviction. Back then, no high could contain the sizzle of my ceaseless energy; few perceived my slow road toward self-medicating, least of all me. So I rode out my winter in the desert, watching the bulldozers break ground on master-planned McMansions, just a few short years before the financial crash that would find most of them foreclosed. Kelly was a semester from graduation, I was going on twenty-one, and the band and I were off to see the world again—this time with our name at the top of the marquee.

Winter of '03. Every tour has its stories, and their sum is a story in itself. I could talk about the blizzard that found us fishtailing sixteen hours down the eastern seaboard to safety or about how our bus driver used to hang out with the band all day instead of sleeping before overnight drives. I could tell you about the co-headlining act whose singer played with his back to the crowd on the nights he felt unloved or about the piano pyrotechnics that ended with a court case in Atlanta and a threat of arrest at customs months later. The snapshots get harder to place in time, but those days we were an arrow, reckless and cutting through the blue skies of early success.

It was our first tour at the top of the bill, and we plowed through the nation beneath its blanket of cold and snow, most days arriving to find a line wrapped around the venue regardless of the weather. Kids under comforters in lumpy jackets, their visible breath slipping through the cracks in their teeth when they smiled. The only reward for their penance was a spot at the barricade and a bladder full of piss, but they paid it without flinching. Idolatry can build soapboxes and dig graves, but the insecure kid housed within my now-grown body saw it as a mantle worthy of respect. I still do. I had been the fan in the front row, I learned the songs of my heroes, bought the merchandise, and waited for autographs in the cold by the backstage door. I needed those lines of waiting strangers wrapped around the building; they validated the life I had chosen for myself and made it possible to go on living it.

When you're clocking real miles, it's easy to believe your troubles belong to yesterday. You wake up each morning in a new city, your worry scattered with last night's gravel in the wake of your tin can on wheels. Someone else makes your bed, empties the trash, and books the hotels. Why shouldn't they solve your problems, too? So you start calling your manager when you're upset with the band, since it's best not to fight before the show. This works for a while, but over time your art and relationships are governed by an increasingly elaborate game of telephone. And then somewhere along the way, the shine starts bleeding off your little democracy, and the worst part is, you don't realize it until it's too late.

Between the rigorous schedule and shifting power dynamics, the cracks in our foundation were forming, but we were moving too fast to patch them. Decisions that had once been easy were becoming contentious, and personalities confined to close quarters were revealing themselves to be less compatible than before. It's not that the five of us didn't love each other or appreciate how lucky we were, but the pressures of business and the absence of privacy were slowly eroding our bond. Even if we had noticed, and I suppose in some ways we did, we had no language for the conversation. We buried our grievances and focused on the good, until the grievances were impossible to ignore.

We finished the North American leg of the tour just before the spring of '03. Having established the band as a bankable closer, we boarded a plane for the UK, hoping to prove the same overseas. We weren't disappointed. There were long lines of teenagers in bootlegged T-shirts, our logo climbing from the cotton in globs of cheap plastisol. Most nights the crowds were louder than the PA, singing every word, whether they spoke the language or not. But as we made our way through the UK and Europe that March, the United States was picking fights in the Middle East, and our tour, which began as a victory lap, fell victim to a heavy mood. Two nights before the invasion of Iraq, I found myself in a hotel room in Leeds, with an eighth of Amsterdam mushrooms and an American band who just happened to be passing through town. My proclivity for escapism had been growing alongside my sense of waning control, and I had found psychedelics to be an effective vacation.

I chewed up the contents of the baggie, muscling through the gag reflex and the queasy aftermath. When the poison took hold, I caught a glimpse of the full moon through the window of the hotel room, and everything else disappeared. I made for the hallway and the lobby on the second floor where a broken escalator stood between me and the dark spring street. I was peaking, my mind obliterated then expanding, everything flexing and layered in shapes. Then a good Samaritan pulled me from the riddle and led me to a staircase and the hotel's front door. The journey was underway.

I followed the full moon through the streets of that gothic hamlet, so certain I could reach it, make it a planet of my own, if I only kept walking. I was of myself but not myself, skirting the line between control and coming apart completely, a world I grew increasingly fond of inhabiting. Everything was spires and burgundy brown, and I tended to the alleys for fear of being discovered. For hours it was the moon and me, only I had no past or future and everything was glass: so very fragile and perfectly clear.

When I rejoined the world, I was lost and unsure of what came next. Shifting into solitary gears, even briefly, is dangerous in a life with so little privacy, but it was too late to go back now. I locked myself in a phone booth, waited for my memory to return, and when it did, I called Arvis, the friend and road manager who would from that day forward be my lifeline. He guided me from the phone booth to the bookstore where my call had found him, and I followed him through the remainder of a quiet night—his calm, like a hand on a kite string, slowly drawing me back to earth.

I rose the next morning with a song in my head and wrote it onstage while the crew unloaded gear and the United States, despite the ire of the world, prepped its invasion of Iraq. My politics had been shaped long before those days, but sitting on foreign soil as my country marched into an unjust war served to clad them in concrete and rage. We played the show that night but it felt criminal, bouncing up and down while politicians sent soldiers to war on a lie. Two days later, the band and I packed our things, canceled the tour, and went home to regroup. I had never backed out of a show before and wouldn't again for another two years, but by then there would be a war at *my* doorstep, and whether it was just or not, I would be required to fight it.

Chapter 18

GLITTERING EXITS

There was an order to how things fell apart. Days of mending fences and days of chasing arrows to the exit doors.

With the mess unfolding overseas, I returned once more to the desert and to our little room with the blue light and bulldozer view. My nerves were shot, but you were steady as ever as we convened our brief rebellion against the zeitgeist. I traded in prevailing tempos and themes, downshifting into the navy mood of life as I was finding it. Those were the last of our guest room adventures, but we did the work and it doubled as good medicine. By the time I boarded a plane heading north to meet the band, you were alone in a room I'd never return to. The movers would come for you without warning, and we'd meet again for one last summer on the road.

♫

Shoreline was the wooded enclave on the outskirts of Seattle where the band and I decamped to record what would end up being Something

Corporate's final album. It was April of '03. We left Los Angeles to avoid distraction, and like a family on the verge of divorce, we took a holiday, hoping the fresh air would remind us how it felt to breathe when things were good and life was less complicated. The house and the studio were haunted, and the owner swung his hammer daily, to satisfy the ghost. Legend had it the whole complex was carved into the hillside decades prior, thanks to a treasure hunt and some dug-up drug money. The man who hid the treasure had perished at the hands of a bike gang, and it was his spirit, we were told, who opened doors we thought we had closed and turned on lights we swore we switched off before bed. But that's another story. I stayed in the crow's nest on the third floor, waking up each morning to a black cat and a view of Puget Sound. The band slept scattered throughout the home's many rooms, and we would gather in the kitchen for morning coffee before descending the staircase to the studio below.

I worked on the new record there for the better part of two months, and with the exception of Josh and our production team, the rest of the band filtered in and out with varying degrees of frequency. I see now, they were giving me the latitude I so clearly desired, but at the time I pitted my commitment against theirs. As bandmates, we had been many things to one another: childhood friends, collaborators, traveling companions, and business partners. We had become men in the process, whatever that means. For a time, success drew us closer together, but by then there was an emerging need to establish ourselves outside of the identity we shared. We moved to different towns and saw one another less off the road. The distance was healthy, it shored us up as individuals, but the farther we traveled from what bonded us the more difficult it became to agree on our future. In the early days, my vision for the band was rarely challenged, but understandably, as it became each member's livelihood, few decisions came up without a vote. I found compromise exhausting, and my desire for control inspired a natural opposition that, over time, left me increasingly isolated. I was too young to see the big picture; I think we all were. Rather than address our frustrations, we bottled them and proceeded in search of quick fixes to keep us moving down the road. In a way, our decision to leave town was rooted in optimism, a vision of us, circled once again around our common cause. For the most part, it worked, but by the time the album was mixed and released, we found ourselves drifting apart again.

I could bore you with the mundane details of our demise, but the truth split in fifths and dosed by its least objective historian would do it little justice. What I can say without fear of rebuke is this: prior to the end of my time in Shoreline, I had a brutal and revelatory hallucination. I chased a quarter ounce of mushrooms down a rabbit hole where I was forced to reckon with my badly injured bloodline. I found my sister there. Her mental illness had spiraled again, landing her in a sick ward for the second time in three years, and I saw my father there, too. He looked just like me, treading water with no land in sight. I wasn't merely a witness to their pain—I was inside it and I couldn't escape. I dialed Kelly in the real world as my fingernails worked to remove the tattoos from my left forearm. She caught me before I hit bottom and, from a thousand miles away, guided me through the labyrinth of my mind. In time, the sun emerged from behind the clouds of gray cotton, and as it did, I climbed onto the roof to watch it fall into the Sound.

When I woke the next morning, it was as if I'd been ripped from a fog. I thought about Ohio for the first time in years, about my father and the crimson door, and I thought about my mother and Stuart and how his death transformed us both. I thought about my older siblings in the water, saved by a man I would never meet, about Kate and her chemistry wars, and Kelly coaching me through the maze the night before. Finally, I thought about the sunset, which drew me to the rooftop, feet dangling, on the other side of wicked hours. There was redemption in that sky on fire.

I descended the stairs to the studio at dawn to find the piano waiting. The song arrived like the rain did so many mornings on Puget

Sound, and like the rain it cleared debris from the boarded-up neighbor-hoods of my heart. I wanted to share what I had written with the band, but by the time the song was finished most of them had returned to California. My frustration with creative democracy was hardly a secret by then, and it's safe to assume they had grown tired of me lording over the control room with my head down. Josh was the exception, but, in the end, he was the one most troubled by my late addition.

Josh had become a talented writer, competing for limited space on our releases. He saw my move to add the song as a land grab and wouldn't sign off without being allowed another track of his own. I respected his position, but didn't care for his song, so I sacrificed mine without a fight. Josh and I had bonded in recent months, even as other members of the band and I had grown distant. I needed his friendship more than the win, so I compromised on the music, but the decision swelled into a private crisis, triggering my instinct for flight.

When the album came out in the fall of '03, my little anthem wasn't on it, left instead to languish as an international B side. William quit shortly after. He and I had stopped spending time together off tour long ago, so when he invited me to lunch just before Christmas, I knew it was the end. I hired a ringer in his place, an old friend of the band's named Bobby Anderson, and took two months off in California to remind myself of who I was and how I had gotten there.

I had a home of my own now, a townhouse in yet another master-planned community. This one was a sea of terra-cotta roofs, barely driven blacktop, and sidewalks lined with twiggy trees in beds of society garlic. Growing up a nomad, I took pride in planting roots so young and paying for that privilege with my songs. Trejo and Daniels moved in while I was still on tour, outfitting the place with floor-bound mat-tresses, a used couch, and a cardboard coffee table. And walking through the door for the first time that winter, I had never felt more at home.

The band and I had recorded and released two full-length albums in less than three years and toured nearly nonstop supporting them.

Exhausted as I was, my friends and I spent those rare months off turning that townhouse into a sanctuary. The repair was nearly immediate. It was there I relearned the mechanics of my own volition, the circadian rhythm of unplanned days. Kelly and I were thriving; she had graduated and moved into an apartment down the street with a friend she'd met in Florence, but she spent most of her nights with me. How she managed to get herself through school and keep me from falling apart completely, sometimes a world away, was a testament to her strength, and in the end would be good practice for the future we'd share. We took to playing house, painting walls, buying furniture, and contemplating marriage. My life without her in it seemed both unlikely and untenable, but when my self-imposed vacation came to an end in the spring of '04, I began to question everything holding me in place. The shows had gotten bigger, and I was caving to the lifestyle, creating distance from my family and making fewer calls home. Around the same time, Kate was back in the hospital again, and rather than find a way to be there for her, I added dates to the schedule, refusing to acknowledge her illness for fear of the giant it might awaken within me.

Then in June, I boarded an airplane for a run of shows in Australia despite the burnout and the promises I had made to come home. The managers were already talking studio time and recording schedules for another album, but I had quietly begun laying the foundation for what would become my monument to independence. I'd clawed my way to the cloud-covered peak of success, and in an act my peers and paid advisers would herald as career suicide, I climbed right back down and started all over again. The selfishness of my twenties was upon me.

Chapter 19

From the Platform, Launch the Submarine

The next time we met I was unrecognizable. It was June of 2004. Kelly drive me from the airport to the pharmacy where I bought a set of cheap clippers so we could shave my head in the garage next to my still-packed suitcase. I was shedding attachments with the subtlety of a wrecking ball. Prior to the album release, the lineup change, and the death knell of too many tours in a row, I commuted your sentence as my road companion and moved you into the townhouse I bought with my first real money. You had lived a life by then, and I have to believe that you were grateful for the quiet bedroom and courtyard view. I know I was.

♪

As they had since childhood, my years began in the summer, and that summer was no different. I had initiated the band's hiatus with a manifesto that I read aloud in an Australian hotel room, voice shaking with tears in my eyes. Those were the first honest words I had marshalled on the topic of friendship, art, and growing up on a road with no map. When I raised my head from the screen to find the faces of my bandmates, I saw myself in them. Ragged and grateful for a little cool water on the wound. It was like I could breathe again, knowing my truth resembled theirs and that we'd simply been too scared to speak the words. It had all been so complicated, but unwinding it was as simple as a finger on a light switch. We would continue to do one-off shows and short tours to pay the bills, but we agreed to cancel plans for recording and to spend some much-needed time at home.

I returned to find you in our room at the top of the stairs, the one with Berber carpet and my first king-size bed. It was like meeting you all over again. Your lid, which didn't latch anymore, left your guts exposed in a gold and mathematic elegance. You fit so perfectly in the corner between the window and the wall it was as if I'd hired an architect strictly for your purposes. This was the room where you would come to life for me. You'd been a prop and a friend in a time when I needed both, but in the months to follow, with the seas-of-self rising, you would become my submarine.

♫

It was not long after Kelly's hand had guided the blade across my skull, erasing what was left of the teenager who first kissed her, that I began the process of setting her free. I was desperate to be alone. Years of cramped quarters and bandmates sleeping feet away on tour buses had finally caught up with me. Nearly every moment of my adult life had been scheduled, and though it had been a beautiful ride, the moment I cut the cord with the band in Australia, I was overwhelmed by a desire to cut more: to disconnect and to find out who I was with no one watching. I had been moving through the world attached to so many: my bandmates, road crew, managers, and, most important, Kelly, but somewhere along the way I'd lost sight of where they ended and where I began. I became impulsive, severing connections, and Kelly got caught up in all of that, through no fault of her own.

Like most love at the finish, it went badly. There were separations and sad mornings after sex that had only made things worse. There were fights in cars at the ends of driveways and phone calls that withered in silence. The summer days we found ourselves drifting through had once been home to our beginning and would soon bear witness to our end. Warm months passed in the shadow of my indecision until I finally placed the call and descended the hill from my little house into the heart of town, where Kelly lived. It was an overcast September day; I met her at her apartment on Granada, and we left from her driveway on foot. We followed the winding streets to the pier at the bottom of hill, its wooden arm stretched out a hundred yards over the Pacific. We walked it all the way to the end. From there, if you stared straight into the horizon without looking down, it almost felt like floating, but that afternoon it was hard to feel anything but loss. All our optimism and negotiations, all the time spent wondering if a little time alone would get us back on track…all of it was over. I had spent weeks assuring her we would be together in the end, and for the first time, despite believing it, I was forced to say *the other thing*. The truth was far too strange, tangled up in years of belonging to a network of souls outside myself. Trying to sell it as such any longer would be unfair to her and might deprive me of the proper free fall I craved. So I told her I was done, that I didn't see a future for us, and that it was best we didn't speak. I walked her up the hill to her apartment, the two of us like ghosts; I said goodbye and drove away, not knowing if I would ever see her again.

Chapter 20

EVERYTHING IN TRANSIT

Music spilled into the courtyard through a crack in the window, and I circled you like an orbiting moon. Those were days of discovery and paying the neighbors no mind. When the chords arrived, the words were never far, riding melodies and rhythms I'd only dreamed of. Other times, the words came first, a phrase of longing or exaltation of the life I'd given myself permission to live. I would sit for hours, hunched over your keys, staring through your abyss of exposed string and wire, holding ideas like fragile bodies until you wrapped them in your armor.

♫

My bedroom became the center of my world. I slept rarely, ate only to survive, and spent my days chasing songs from that room to the studio speakers. I felt Kelly like a phantom limb, but for all my longing, I was more alive than ever, stretching out in all directions with time to kill and money to burn. The paradox of my chosen broken heart.

I was twenty-two. Living to write, writing to record, and recording to document the changes taking place around me and within. The more I wrote, the more time I spent at the studio on Fourth Street in Santa Monica, a block from the shops on the promenade. It was as much a home to me as anywhere. The space was a long rectangular box, broken into three small rooms, each buffered by a pair of heavy doors. There was an office up front with stickers on the windows, gold records on the walls, and a desk covered with bills it was safe to assume were past due. Next was the tracking room, the largest of the three, with its parquet floors, a ceiling like a rolling wave, and a seven-foot grand piano pressed against the wall; one of the finest-sounding instruments I had ever played. Last was the control room, a shoebox packed with gear and wrapped in walls of dark velvet, sequestering decades of smoke and history. Kathleen Wirt, the owner, was a tall bohemian, always worried about money, Republicans, and the weed fog that escaped into the hall they shared with a children's theater. She treated me and all who passed through her door like family, including the man who called Fourth Street home, her ex-husband and my producer, Jim Wirt.

Jim had recorded nearly every note of Something Corporate's released music. When I met him, he was little more than a cartoon character to me, but his humanity revealed itself with time as our creative bond grew. He was long limbed, thin, and carried himself like a rag doll with his shoulders hunched forward, leading with the crown of his head. He had a drawl by way of Missouri and a baby girl with a woman back home. Jim was convinced his safety and salvation could be found between the speakers, and the farther we got into the recording of the album we began work on that summer, the more inclined I was to agree with him.

We would commune after hours for a discounted rate. I would play Jim the songs I had written since we had last seen each other, he would pick his favorite, and I'd lay down the piano and vocals in a few takes. For most of the sessions it was just the two of us and an engineer, and in the absence of a band our work became an experiment born of necessity. We made beats from chopped-up drum loops, and we danced in the control room, grabbing instruments and charging back and forth to the microphones. And by the end of each session, which often placed me on the road just before sunrise, I'd be traveling home with a brand-new song. The process was as natural as breathing, and I came to crave it like a body does oxygen.

Things were moving fast again, the way they do at the beginning when you're hungry and the businesspeople bet on you. A batch of the songs we cut in those late-night sprints ended up in just enough hands to cause a stir, and by the fall of '04, I had signed a new record deal. The sense of destiny that had buoyed me throughout my realignment with the world was now fixed to the machinery of commerce. Suddenly, there was a team dedicated to my reinvention, a project I went on to call Jack's Mannequin.

Chapter 21

Grief for the Living, No Really, I'm Fine

My father went back to rehab in September of '04. It was a short stay, and I feigned support for the effort while juggling my own personal sea change. I had barely been in touch with my family prior to the news, despite living just miles away in a neighboring town. We weren't fighting or estranged, I made no conscious effort to avoid them, but I was busy piloting my own adventures in excess and allowed my family to be swept up in the same house cleaning that jettisoned my love and bandmates. Less than a month later, my grandfather on my dad's side passed away.

I don't remember getting the phone call, but I remember the dread I felt boarding the plane to New Jersey. I barely knew the man I was traveling to grieve or the wife he had left behind. Whether this had been my father's intention, his lack of effort to the contrary provided for little else. Had my grandparents been aware of what our family had survived? I imagine they had, and that our relationships fractured along the fault lines of my father's disease, but outside of birthday cards and holiday phone calls, they were strangers to me.

The trip was surreal. There were shared meals and a visit to my father's boyhood home, where, for a time, we spent Sundays when I was little. And then there was the service. My mother, father, and Kate, and my sister Emily and I, sat shoulder to shoulder on conference room chairs as a procession of my uncle Doug's friends paid their respects. Whatever my parents and Kate had weathered in my years of nonstop touring was as foreign to me as the man on display. I had become an outsider in their world. They would have preferred otherwise. In a way, I would have, too, but I had pulled the drawbridge years before, and though we could shout across the distance, I had forgotten how to reach the other side.

I stared into space, past the flowers and the open casket of a father whose son had stopped visiting long ago, and I grieved, not for his passing, but for what was passing in our midst. Had this scene played out for generations, was it wrapped up in my blood? Would I, one day, bring heirs with barriers between us to mourn a man I didn't let them know? Or would I allow the surname I had been tasked to carry on reach its dead end with me and stop the bleeding?

Before we left, my uncle Doug took me to the room inside the VA where my grandfather spent his final years. Doug was a good man with a Jersey accent and a gambling habit. Not the kind that gets you into trouble with a bookie, but the kind that finds you killing time in Atlantic City on the weekends, coming home no worse for the wear. He looked like a version of my father in flaxen hair and white tennis shoes. Doug had taken care of his parents, and my family had done little to support his efforts. Why, I couldn't say. It seemed to me a shameful abdication, but if he harbored any resentments, he hid them well.

In my grandfather's room there were keepsakes of undisclosed meaning parked next to pictures of my siblings and me, but it was what lay hidden in the desk drawers beside his neatly made bed that I found most compelling: a stack of journals filled with a script so delicate, they could have been the work of a watchmaker. I looked to Doug for permission, which he granted with a nod, as if to say, *this was your grandfather, I'm sorry you barely knew him.* In death, he reached for me from pages not unlike the ones I was filling those days. The unpublished philosophy of a man who owned some piece of me. And in reading his words, I was reminded of the vast coded rivers that powered my existence. The faceless generations that came before. I found comfort in the mystery, a sense that being tied to so many I would never know freed me from belonging to anyone. I had become an expert at extracting the meaning I needed from the things I couldn't control. When the ritual was complete, I spent the night in an airport hotel, then boarded a plane home to my piano and my friends, shaken, but still on course.

The rest of the fall, my days of motion met little resistance. Trejo, Daniels, and I would get restless at midnight and drive to Vegas; I'd spend my Fridays at Fourth Street and then crash with my agent for a weekend bender. And with no one looking in on me, I was even more free to experiment than I had been before. Pot was still my go-to fix, but I was no stranger to harder drugs. I enjoyed playing at the boundaries' edges, chipping away at the guardrails, anything to prove I answered to no one. After our months-long breakup, Kelly and I had kept our word and stopped calling, but with every mile I traveled, she was never far away. At home behind the keys of my piano, it was her I wrote about, and when the writing was done and I was back at Fourth Street, it was our story playing out in the speakers. I couldn't tell if I was working out our ending or writing my way back to her, but all the suffering and wonder pulled me farther down a path with few obstacles. So I pressed on.

In November the band and I broke our hiatus, set sail on a money run, and without the usual pressures of promotion and creative deadlines, the walls came down and we played dangerously again. Before the business of music, we had been friends in a garage, and our return to the road reminded me of the days when we cared but didn't hold on too tight. By then I had gotten close with Bobby, the guitarist we had hired to fill the vacancy left by William's departure the year before. We called him "Raw," and he honored the name with his antics both onstage and off. At over six feet, with fair skin and ash-blond hair, it was a little like taking the stage with a Viking—one who slept late, played hard, and spoke with an untraceable accent that became a mouth full of marbles when he drank too much. In December he would join me at Fourth Street, where together we'd finish my album of songs about lost love and late nights in bars with friends. It would be everything I had hoped to make since first stepping through a studio door, but its release would find me on my mortal edge, too sick to meet the wind that had carried me there.

Chapter 22

Walls of Rain

Winter of '04, '05. The days were drenched in rain, a historic winter downpour gunning for a century-old record. California was drowning, but like every ringing phone and traffic light those days, I believed that it was a sign, and signs were not to be questioned. I rented a place in Beverly Hills in December and left Trejo and Daniels to care for the townhouse while I worked. My depleted bank account had been made whole again, with the tab for the album now being picked up by the new record company. For months, I had been commuting to Fourth Street, and with the influx of cash, I opted for a little convenience. A place to lay my head down between sessions. The apartment was an upgrade from the crash pads I had rented for previous records—a corner unit in a complex called The Versailles. There was a black leather couch with metal legs and a platform bed in a room with no dresser. Austerity parading as minimalist design. From the windows, just beyond my alley view, was Robertson Boulevard, a street of overpriced retail shops, where the stretched and injected squandered their fortunes daily. Raw flew in for the month, and I let him have the bedroom. My insomnia required a switched-on television and the apartment had only one, so I camped out in the living room, where, on good nights, it sang me to sleep.

We were a skeleton crew on a mission. Jim and I with our shared brain, Raw with his guitar, and our engineer, CJ, whose job it was to wrangle our output into listenable music. It was Christmas in Santa Monica, but aside from the occasional break spent gazing at the lights in the trees on the promenade, the holiday would go unnoticed. The four of us entered the trench daily, building up the canvas of each song, listening back, and then moving on to the next. We kept acid in the fridge but never took it and set up microphones in the hallway to record the sound of the rain. Long studio days dovetailed into nightcaps at Finn McCool's in Venice or Renee's in Santa Monica, but with few exceptions, we worked seven days a week around the clock, without a worry for the world outside.

Months before, I had been working in the studio with Jim when I got a surprise phone call from Tommy Lee, the drummer of Mötley Crüe. The sound of his surfer slang was a time machine, transporting me back to a childhood spent parked on couches for hours watching MTV. I'll never forget that call. I clasped one hand over the receiver, pointing at the phone with the index finger of my other, mouthing Tommy's name across the control room to Jim. We were wrapped up, as we had been all summer, in my music with no set destination, but somehow, we knew that call was a sign of good things to come. Tommy had gotten his hands on a copy of Something Corporate's final album, *North*, and had been listening to my song about chasing the moon—the one I'd written onstage in Leeds before the war broke out. He was working on a new album of his own and writing a song he hoped I would help him finish. An hour later, I was driving through the Hollywood hills on my way to the first of our many sessions together, work that continued into that rain-swept December.

Tommy was one of the most passionate musicians I had ever met. I would finish in Santa Monica and then drive to Hollywood, where we would write and record at his producer's house, a modern concrete box that hugged a cliff in the famed Nichols Canyon. His universe was intoxicating. A night in the studio would start with some legendary story about famous friends or an international DJ gig ending in a high-speed chase. From there, we'd listen to music or work on a track, and when Tommy liked what he heard, his ink-covered arms became visual rhythm, and his joy could not be contained. We would record for a few hours and then a chef would arrive with a bunch of prerolled joints, which we'd smoke in preparation for dinner. Tommy could elevate the frequency of a room the way I had only seen my uncle Stuart do before him; the impact of our intermittent sessions, along with his belief in me as a writer, was yet another signal to keep pushing ahead.

I finished tracking the new album just before Christmas. In our final week, having played most of the music for Tommy, he agreed to make a guest appearance. True to form, he turned the night into a drum clinic and, one after another, he tackled nearly every track on the album. Suddenly, my little record of chopped up-loops was under the influence of one of rock's most iconic drummers. I was on the runway with an engine full of jet fuel, and there was only one way to go. Up.

All the living I had done had been collected and then reimagined as sound. And with Raw on a plane back to Virginia, I returned to my house and my roommates and news of Kelly's plans to leave California. Months apart had left her in search of new vistas, and when the holidays were through, she would join family on the East Coast in a town with no memory of us. I threw a blowout on New Year's Eve at my parents' house, a nod to simpler times, and invited Kelly, knowing it might be the last chance we would have to see each other. By the time she arrived, I had turned my body into a chemistry set, and the evening went south before midnight. Our magnets still worked on each other, and Kelly used hers to peel me from the ceiling. For a time, the party raged around our sinking ship, and then the party became a sinking ship itself. Happy New Year two thousand and five. In the morning, I wrote my goodbyes to her on the old upright in my parents' garage, the one I played in the early days of Something Corporate, with the tour dates tattooed on its shell in Sharpie marker. Just as I finished the song, she showed up at the house, rattled by the way we had left things. We agreed, it hadn't been the ending we had hoped for—and made plans to try again later that week.

I pulled into Kelly's driveway a few days later during yet another winter storm, and she ran out into the downpour to meet me. I cranked the heat to help her clothes dry and eased my car onto the road like a boat on a river. My last memory of such pile-driving rain, I was sixteen. My car was top heavy, the tires bald, and my mother shouted commands at me from the passenger seat in the run-up to us somersaulting down the freeway. That crash was the first time I understood the frailty of the physical world and my place within it; since then, I have abhorred the task of driving in the rain.

I skipped the interstate and took side streets to the movie theater, the safest place to kill hours when you've lost all the right words. I couldn't remember the last time Kelly and I had driven together. I'd done so much living since then, and though I wanted to tell her everything, the few words I didn't choke on were no match for the torrent lashing the windows and the roof. When we finally arrived, I dropped her at the front of the theater and caught my breath, alone inside my car beneath an avalanche of falling water. I thought briefly about the surrounding darkness that would, on most days, be hours from its descent. Something about being together at night felt impossible, but the night found us anyway.

Soaked at the box office window, I bought two tickets for the *Garden State* matinee, and we proceeded to the theater with its rows of red fabric seats. Why we chose that movie is beyond me, but the parallels to our story were uncanny, and it made those hours in the dark a chore. We fidgeted against instinct, pulses on roller coaster rails, hands almost reaching for hands. There was something about sitting in that theater that made me wish I'd never left her. I found myself wishing for a stitched-up ending and pitch-perfect soundtrack playing as the credits rolled. But there with Kelly, the two of us rail thin from the fallout of our split, it seemed to me that our reunion would require more time.

Gut punched, we drifted from the theater to the lobby, eyes adjusting first to the light and then to the waterfall encircling everything. Kelly waited while I ran to the car, one final chivalrous deed. On the ride from her house, I was sure I had never traveled under more relentless skies, but after the movie, with her in the passenger seat, both of us shaking in a skin of rain, the gods found one more level and pushed down like holy hell. This was our storm now; driving would be suicide. I inched through the floodwaters into a space and parked my car, the one we used to drive stoned to the Dairy Queen. There were words beneath the surface for both of us, but we couldn't locate them, so we just stared out into the storm. And for the first time since I had pulled into her driveway that afternoon, we laughed. There was justice in *this* ending. The natural order had been upset, and the time was coming soon when we would need to set things right.

Chapter 23

DARK BLUE

I'm outside my body, looking down from a navy-and-star-filled sky. A town rises from the coastline, my town, wrapped in a sheet of moonlight and blue. I scan the terrain. Inland, where the hillside peaks, a singular being stares out toward the ocean, rising. Recognition. I am the watcher and the watched. The chaos begins with the wind. Palm trees flex in unison, a ballet on closing night. Tiles loosen on rooftops, cars shimmy on their troubled axles, and a single wave as wide as the horizon advances east. From the hilltop and the sky, my separated selves merge. We are moments from the moment. The physical universe explodes, first before me and then around. The shrapnel of existence: plants and people, road signs, books and tires. Stillness descends as I am claimed by the wave. I try swimming to the surface, but in the absence of a guiding light I go slack, accepting my fate in a shipwrecked town. There is nothing more to do. Then, without warning, fate has other plans for me, and I am thrust to the surface of deep water on a summer night. The concrete and sprawl, the shopping centers and cliffside mansions, have all been erased by the wave. In the stillness of starlight my eyes begin to work again...there is someone in the water with me. With no plans left to make, no fear or hunger pains, just peace and faith in floating, the magnets do their work, returning me to the girl with the green eyes.

I wake up and we write the ending.

♫

Jack's Mannequin left for tour in the spring of '05. The moniker I had assumed was now a band. Raw took on the role of my second in command, and I drew heavily on his contacts to complete the line-up. JayMac was my first call. A human metronome, raised in the sticks of Virginia, his drumming reflected his way of life: deliberate and unadorned. In those days, his hair shot up and out in a mop of curls that defied orders when he played, but regarding everything else, JayMac was always in control. I had toured with him when Something Corporate was just starting out, and he and Raw played together in a band out of Richmond, Virginia. They took an early interest in us, passing on their mantle of party tricks and road wisdom, and we looked up to them like older brothers. While the remainder of the lineup would have to audition, I knew what JayMac was capable of and offered him the gig over the phone.

Word of our formation had made its way through Richmond to a bass player friendly with my new bandmates. I thought it impractical to hire another player from out of state, so I passed, but he booked a flight anyway, showing up with his bass and the clothes on his back. He was thin, childlike, dressed in a Celtics jersey and vintage sneakers, with an asymmetrical rope of long hair hanging over one eye. Like Raw, he had an unplaceable accent, and combined with his tendency to trail off at the ends of his sentences, half of what he said was a mystery. His name was Jon, but we called him Dr. J, and he played bass just as well as he hustled. We practiced for an afternoon, then the four of us hit the bars together. Plastered at the night's end, I offered him the job in a Burger King on Sunset Boulevard, where he had just gotten into a fist fight with a hamburger.

Finally, there was Jacques, an LA-based guitarist with hipster bona fides and a Rolodex of famous friends. Somehow, he managed to moonlight as a professional photographer when he wasn't on the road, and he was just as skilled behind a camera as he was in front of an amp. The five of us holed up in a rehearsal space in the valley and over the course of a month prepared for the tour, during which time Jacques proved himself to be as valuable a social director as he was a musician. We weren't just starting a band; we were building a party machine.

The first show of the tour was on Cinco de Mayo in the basement of a Bakersfield pizza parlor. A dungeon with a single power strip hanging from the ceiling that you plugged into at your own peril. Well aware of the stigma associated with "going solo," I resisted leveraging my name to sell tickets. Instead, we hit the message boards, leaking songs and rumors about the project, hoping fans would find their way to the shows. We played to six people that first night, sharing the bill with Josh from Something Corporate and the new band he was fronting. And while the show was a far cry from the tour bus and the sold-out clubs we were used to, it was exactly where I wanted to be. There was something poetic in that sendoff, being able to watch Josh from the crowd as a fan, in a room just like the ones we had grown up playing together. I loved his songs. We had struggled at times to navigate the waters we shared, but that night I felt a sense of pride, not for what we created, but for the friendship that made it possible to release each other into new frontiers. When the work was done, we hit the bars and, like most responsible adults, ended the night launching construction signs into an aqueduct on the way back to the motel.

From Bakersfield, the band and I headed north, playing dives from the Bay Area to Portland. Our experiment seemed to be working, with the curious crowds growing nightly. By the time we returned to Los

Angeles, word of the band had spread, and we unpacked our gear at the legendary Troubadour to news of a sellout.

When I stepped onto the stage that night, I was well aware of its legacy. Elton John had famously made his US debut there, and I sweat it out beneath the blue neon sign bearing the club's name, hoping to earn my place in its history. Bootlegs of the first few shows had surfaced, and the audience arrived having done their homework. The label was impressed; the evening was electric and pure. When it was over, we packed the trailer and spilled out into the street in pursuit of some ritual release. Two mornings later, the band and I woke up on my agent's floor, and having missed our alarm, we raced toward Arizona, nursing hangovers from a weekend of bar tabs charged to company cards.

We made it to Tucson before soundcheck, parked the van, and listened to the Everly Brothers in the rain. Kelly was never far from my mind those days, but always closer when the skies opened up or a sad song played. Months had passed since we'd seen each other, but we were speaking again. I'm not sure if it was the weather or the light at play inside the hotel when we finally made our way through the front door, but there was a cinematic thread woven through the fabric of that day—a cradle of foreboding and calm, and to hold that space was to miss her even more.

The Hotel Congress was a historic dive, a shabby love letter to its heritage, with Spanish tiles on the floor and wood-paneled walls trimmed in Southwestern oranges and blues. There was a small stage off the lobby, which meant the show, the afterparty, and the bad night's sleep would all play out under the same roof. A rare and perfect storm. By sundown, the humidity had made its way from the outside in, preserving the show in a sweat-drenched memory. I said my thank-yous to the crowd and returned to my room having sung enough songs about love and longing to know where I stood on the matter.

I threw on some dry clothes and found my way to the lobby, where I was greeted by the band and a pill. It was ecstasy, and it hit me like a brick. I rode out the onslaught in a bathroom stall, trying not to puke or lose myself. I had never done the drug before and immediately regretted the decision, but there was no turning back now. When I was well enough to stand, I found Raw at the bar. He could tell I was in trouble and shouldered me back to the room. Propped up on the headboard, I waited for the transformation while he strummed an acoustic in the corner. My condition was getting worse. I was up against it now—the fear I had pushed myself too far and the wishing it was over. The dark arms of panic were tightening around me. Then just as I was coming apart, the moment of profound chemistry arrived on the back of a Beethoven quartet. When he had sensed I was approaching the peak, Raw had insisted I focus on his laptop and the classical piece he had chosen to distract me from the chaos. It didn't matter if his speakers were trash or that I'd been sick just seconds before. The music built on itself, then gathered in my blood, my heartbeat like a medicine drum. I'd never heard a more perfect song, and with its strings fixed to my limbs and its breath to my lips, it pulled me from the fear and shaking and launched me back into the world. A pinball set free in the hallways.

Raw had saved me, the guardian with his guitar, his laptop, and library of classical music. And with the danger now a distant memory, the night began. I roamed the hotel searching for open doors and found songwriters on bed edges hunched over guitars. Downstairs there were friends and strangers clustered beneath the pale orange lights of the lobby bar, laughing on a shared frequency. In flight now, sweat gathering just below the surface of my skin, I had all but forgotten the violent journey to that place. Little did I know that the extremity of my condition was the foreshadowing of a war. Enemy cells were dividing into armies more powerful than the systems within me they aimed to destroy. My blood was compromised, and time was running out.

Perhaps it was my subconscious at work, the triggering of early warnings, demanding I tie up loose ends. Maybe it was the serotonin cut loose without a flood wall. Whatever the reason, I knew where I needed to be and called Kelly from the bar. She was back in California for the month, gathering her things for a permanent move to the East Coast. There were two days off before the next show in Ohio, and I would have time to fly home. Would she see me if I did? I reached for my phone, doing what I could to control the pill controlling me, but Kelly was no stranger to my after-hours persona by then. I'd been wasted or hungover on most of our calls that month. It was hard to catch me any other way. While I hadn't solved that problem yet, I couldn't be without her any longer, and when she agreed to see me, I booked my flight home still reeling from the drug. I drank until the bar closed, and when it did, I hitched a ride with friends to Phoenix and the Sky Harbor airport.

You were waiting for me in the early morning light. I showered off the drinks, my anticipation overriding their attempts to drag me down. Emerging from the closet in fresh clothes to take you in for the first time since landing, I sensed our yearlong adventure was nearing its conclusion. I had found what I was looking for: a life where making things was painless even if the living was not, a second chance at the dream I'd let become a burden, and a love even I could not destroy with all my recklessness and curiosity. Whether Kelly would take me back I wasn't sure, but the road to her felt good beneath my feet, and if I only got to walk it, that was something. Looking back at you as I stepped through the doorway, I couldn't help but think—everything was about to change.

♫

Chapter 24

So Long Mr. Invincible

May 27, 2005. I'm in a taxi heading east through Central Park. A Jamaican cabbie with a thick accent, and dreads pinned up in a tam, sings to the radio while my eyes shift in and out of focus. A vintage Land Camera rests in my lap while a scribbled address on scrap paper twitches in my upturned hand. And like so many leaves on the trees outside, the letters shake on the branches of my fingers. If only this were fall and I could shed that beastly foliage, but it's spring and these strange flowers will bloom.

The future had been mine just minutes before. I had been in Chelsea in a concrete high-rise, kneeling one last time at the altar of the record I'd made, the final chapter of my coming of age set to music. Jim had always told me we were safe between the speakers, and that afternoon, like so many before it, I believed him. I listened to the album from beginning to end; it was finished, the transitions and track list confirmed. I signed off and made my way to the street.

The last show was on Long Island. We were coming off sellouts in Philadelphia and New York City. For two nights I celebrated, putting my days of fevers and chattering teeth out of mind with hopes of finding health in the morning. I'd known something was wrong since Columbus. The time at home with Kelly had turned the wheel on our reconciliation, but the flight back to the tour was when everything else began falling apart. During the layover, my lungs quit pushing oxygen, leaving me gasping at the airport walls. I told myself it was the schedule, the late nights, the drugs and drinking, and for the next eight days stood by while my systems shut down. I knew what was happening, not in practical terms, but I could sense that my body was dying.

I didn't agree to see a doctor until the lack of oxygen finally claimed my voice and I was forced to cancel a show. When the bloodwork came back the next day, the results drove a wedge between my first twenty-two years and everything thereafter. They were only words at first, my confusion sought to destroy their meaning, but my denial was as useless as my immune system. The doctor said it plain, then gave me an address; there would be a team waiting for me at the hospital. I grabbed my camera and hurried out into the sparkling, unfortunate day.

The rest was weightlessness and resignation, sterile halls and exam tables lined with cold wax paper. There was no intake form or insurance collected, no next of kin named, or boxes of symptoms checked—just a doctor, some nurses, and me in a room full of machines. I sensed they knew what I was facing and only aimed to confirm it, but one thing was clear: I wasn't leaving. Soon my head was swimming in a foreign vocabulary, words I'd lived my whole life never needing to know. But it wasn't the words, it was the worry in the doctor's eyes that summoned my fear.

Then, like a symphony rising to the height of tension, all the stethoscope breaths and leading questions culminated in a proper act of barbarism, one that found me on my stomach with a needle like a drill bearing down into my hip. The bone marrow biopsy. When the procedure began, I traveled inward searching for my breath. How I knew it would be the only thing to save me, I'm not sure, but the longer I lay conquered, unmoving, subhuman, the deeper I drew from the bellows attempting to prove that I was not. When it was over, they left me in the room alone, initiated: mourning the death of invincible days. My mind raced. What was this thing in me? What had I done to myself?

I'd spent a year barely eating or sleeping, taking every pill and powder passed my way. Smoking cigarettes and pot interchangeably through-out my eighty-hour workweek. It's hard to explain how much I stood to lose, without understanding how much the music I'd been making meant to me. I had walked away from success, from my band of high school friends, from Kelly and from my family, all for the sake of those songs. Not for their making, but for what their making represented. I had understood the rare moment I was in, that I had arrived at the peak of my creativity, and I purposefully stripped myself bare to embrace it. I had chosen to start over when it would have been easier to stay, and I deployed my craft like a camera into the heart of heartbreak, friend-ship, and the magic of being young. And as I lay in that cold room waiting for a direction, I couldn't help but think—*I followed my music to that hospital. Every cord I cut, every sign that drew me farther down the path I'd been traveling, had landed me in that exam room beneath those fluorescent lights. The table where my hip throbbed now like a body with a heartbeat of its own was no less my destiny than the stage or the studio I had sped away from in a cab just hours before. Whatever crisis I was in the midst of was a part of the design; I don't know how I knew it, but I did.*

I couldn't call Kelly, not yet. I couldn't call my family; they would get on a plane. So I called Jami instead. I needed a friend who knew all of me. And it was on that call I uttered the ugly word out loud for the first time. *Leukemia.* It hung like death and accelerant somewhere over America, caught between the satellites and cell towers connecting us on opposite coasts. There it sat in the center of the panic, and for a moment we shared it, crying together the way you do when you know something is lost forever. I still think of how unfair it was to lay that call on her, to drag her into my nightmare when she was free of me, but the hatchet I had used to clean house left me so few places to turn. How do you tell the people you stopped talking to that all your big plans have blown up in your face?

Speaking the words made it real, and when the call ended, I spent the next few moments alone, auditioning the gravity of my situation. The speed with which I had been moving through the world was untenable, and I had finally hit the wall. Staring at the massive obstacle before me, certain of the path that led me there, I downshifted through my confusion and grief and dialed my father at home. I outlined my predicament, leaning on best-case scenarios, but it was hard to do without setting off alarms. The results of the biopsy would come back in the following days, and under no circumstance was he or my mother to travel until I'd received them. It was a test. I was descending into chaos and still looking for a reason to trust him. I couldn't face my parents in a hospital room. I'd been shaped from the clay of our family disease, raging since youth against the necessity of their care, and I couldn't bear the thought of needing them. Not yet.

Next came the gown, the bracelet, and the wheelchair: affectations of the imprisoned sick. Then I was installed in a room and plugged into machines I knew nothing about. The view was impressive, and in any other building it would have fetched millions. As I stared out at the skyline of windows, some extinguished and black, others lit up, gold and pulsing, I thought about my band, drunk in the bars below. We would have been in some basement together by then, raising glasses to the finished album, to the sold-out shows and our set trajectory, but time had slowed, and from the lethargy, I drew meaning. All the running left me tired, my hunger begat hunger, and the pursuit of myself had found me sleepless in a bed, alone.

In a tangle of wires, I called Kelly from the dark. She caught me as she always did, assuring me I'd pull through whatever it was I was facing, and the way she spoke I believed her. As fate would have it, she was scheduled to board a flight to New York City for a job interview the following day. Yet another testament to magnets and destiny. She agreed to change her return and stay with me while I waited for the news; though she deserved better than a reconciliation in a hospital bed, it seemed we had no other choice. *She* did, I suppose, but even in my wandering year, our love seemed inevitable, and whether it was fair or not, I knew she felt the same. I'd spent the months without her, tallying signs, believing my path affirmed. I followed those signs to my best music, to my identity reclaimed, and to an airport the week before it all fell apart to spend my last healthy day in her arms. We hung up, and as I found myself wishing for sleep, one more signal came hurtling into view. The friend I had named my band after, the Jack in Jack's Mannequin, was a childhood leukemia survivor. It all made sense to me. Just another mile marker on the road I was meant to travel. My faith was intact, the future laid out before me. Everything was aligned.

Here we go.

Chapter 25

WOMEN

I'm living in a waiting room on the 10th floor
    of a New York City skyscraper
I've got the paperwork filled out my friend
Can you tell me how this story ends?

Welcome to the memory-thieving wilderness, with its disinfectants and machine animals cloying at the remembrance of a time you didn't need them. The Jamaican nurses rounded every few hours, hanging bags of blood and saline while I stared out at the buildings, revisiting the events of hours past. There is no sleeping in a hospital without drugs, and I hadn't yet realized I could ask for them. The coming days would require a plan. Arvis would show up in the morning with my keyboard, and we'd hold each other crying in the doorway. Kelly and I would reunite in the afternoon, at times, finding ourselves so wrapped up in each other we'd forget how much trouble I was in. Later that night my family would arrive, despite my protestations, but I would have no energy left for the fight. Eventually, my managers and the record company would fly into town, and together we would decide the fate of my album. The tour would be canceled, and the band sent home.

The diagnosis came on Tuesday. By then, my body was a war zone, and my patience was running thin. The doctor stood at the foot of my bed, and my mother sat in a chair beside me. I knew what was coming; I had seen it in his eyes the day we met—but knowing didn't prepare me for the moment my sentence was handed down. There was a shattering, a thunderclap, and a tear in the fabric of what was and should have been. And when it was over, all I could do was stare at my hands—simultaneously pale and needle bruised. How useful they once had been. It was too much for my mother, and she left the room, destroyed. She had traveled there with her blinders and her hope. I knew she would, and that it wasn't what I needed, and found myself wishing she had stayed home.

It was just as the doctor had suspected, acute lymphocytic leukemia, commonly known as ALL. A cancer of the blood. It renders white cells ineffective, throwing systems into failure and corrupting healthy immune responses. I was an uncommon case, a young man with a disease found mostly in children and older adults. Protocols were in debate, outcomes a coin toss, and there would be no clear path forward. I wanted to run. I had to get out of the city and back to California, but flying without an immune system was too dangerous. The doctor was ready with the chemo and I was ready to fight, but not there. I pressed him for a way out, but my only hope of getting home was a private plane, so I started making phone calls and asked him to find me a hospital with an open bed. My mother thought the plan was far-fetched, that I was being unrealistic, and when she began quietly moving chess pieces in the opposite direction, Kelly confronted her, and all hell broke loose.

For years Kelly had been family; she was Kate's best friend and worked alongside my mother at the Blue Lantern since high school, but our breakup had taken its toll on her, and, in our time apart, she had taken leave of our overlapping worlds. Sadly, my sister got wrapped up in all that. Kate had been hospitalized that year for another bipolar episode, and my mother resented Kelly for not being at her side the way she had been before. It was an awful situation, and if there was anyone to blame it was me, but to blame me would force a reckoning, so my mother chose Kelly instead.

They were in the common room, and I was in a trench of deep sleep. My mother, in her need for control, had begun laying out the next steps—finding a replacement at work and moving in with my sister Emily in New York so she could assume the role as my advocate. When Kelly stepped in on my behalf—knowing this wasn't the plan I'd set in motion—my mother grew enraged, with all her misplaced anger boiling over. She accused Kelly of being an outsider, citing her absence from our lives that year. Kelly gave her grace, understood what my mother was going through, but she wouldn't cosign the insurrection. It was fights like these that I'd been hoping to avoid when I requested my family stay home. But that time had passed, and rather than argue, I focused on the task at hand. While my agent and manager hunted for a private plane, I consulted with the doctor once more, imploring him to find me a West Coast bed, and this time he understood I was serious. It took a day, but it was done.

Loaded into an SUV with three women at odds, I left the war room for the war. Dr. Feldman, my New York oncologist, had a colleague in Los Angeles whom he trusted; his name was Gary Schiller, and despite a full caseload, he agreed to take me on. I was dressed in real clothes for the first time since I had been admitted. It had only been a week, and already they hung from my body like hand-me-downs, but anything was better than the backless gown and blue hospital scrubs I had been passing the days in. With my humanity briefly restored, I met the plane on the tarmac to begin my journey home.

In all my dreams of stardom and private jets, never once did I imagine *that* flight. I scanned the cabin as we taxied to the runway under a blanket of low clouds. To my right was Kelly with her heart still mending, our fingers twisted up like roots, and between us and the cockpit door, my mother and sister with their blonde hair and nervous tics firing. These women would be the bedrock on which I would take my stand. Each would do everything in their power to incubate my slide into the unknown, but no one would do for them what they did for me. The fact that there was so much unsettled between us would be a footnote in the months to come. So much would go unsaid, but for a time we would hover in the present, doing only what needed to be done. The past was irrelevant for now; it was time to get my house in order.

Chapter 26

Crewcuts and Pneumonia

The plane felt like it was coming apart over Kansas. The pilots, blindsided by a summer storm, threw open the cockpit door, demanding calm and seatbelts, then guided the small jet from the atmosphere to earth in minutes. On the tarmac, it was clear that the incident had taken a toll on my fellow passengers, but staring out at the gray sky that had followed me through seasons, I was more certain than ever we would make it home. There was no way I was dying in a plane crash.

We refueled, and after the pilots' thorough inspection—and the repeating of a few dozen Hail Marys by my mother—we completed our journey to Los Angeles and the UCLA Medical Center. My hospital room there was no different than the previous one or any of the others I'd occupy over the next several months. The scents and the sound of machinery clung to me like postblackout hangovers, like guilt and well-kept secrets.

I met Dr. Schiller in the impatient hours, after things had settled and all that was left was urgency: for my treatment to begin, and for some fight to be assigned to those days. He was an assassin in a starched white coat, with every dark hair on his head combed into place and every fingernail trimmed to perfection. If he was half as invested in my care as he was in his diction and appearance, I would be in good hands. His team would confirm my diagnosis with another needle to the hip and a long weekend spent waiting, but I could see palm trees from my hospital window, and whatever came next, at least I was home.

I spent the next few days getting my affairs in order, returning phone calls, writing letters, and banking my sperm because the chemo would render me infertile. And on Saturday morning, with Kelly's head resting on my chest as it had on better days, we decided to exercise what little control over my condition we had left. We dispatched of my hair with the same set of clippers used in my garage the previous summer, our time apart now propped up by crewcut bookends. It was a painful and preemptive "fuck you," and as she pulled the razor across my scalp, shedding the hair I dyed black in her absence, I sensed a strength in her with which I had yet to be acquainted. A conviction that bordered on prophecy. My body was falling apart, so I clung to hers. Her chestnut hair and freckled skin, her slender frame like a harbor in a storm. And with my head cradled in her hands and her lips on my skull, the worst of what lay ahead could do little to disturb the depth of love I felt for her. We were kids when we met, but kneeling on the floor of that hospital bathroom, undeterred by my undoing, was a woman more powerful than any I'd known.

June 8, 2005: "It comes to me now through a hole in my arm, the sweet blue medicine like antifreeze as I wait for more visitors. They come with their concern, their nerves and distaste for hospitals in tow. I've seen all types of visitors, some are bright like hot metal, others pale as the sheets on my bed. My blood pumps slow, my pulse visible in every inch of skin. The nausea comes and goes and occasionally my stomach itches from the antibiotics. I am a sick man, but I am alive. My visitors will be here soon."

High-dose chemotherapy is designed to destroy, and it does its job well. Mine started on a Tuesday. The poison goes to work on your cells and, in turn, your humanity. The closer you inch toward death, the less your body belongs to you and the more essential your spirit becomes. When your blood counts crash, the mouth sores begin and eating becomes intolerable. When the eating stops, you drink your meals, but you are never full. The headaches arrive, followed by the rashes, and depending on the day and the drugs used to combat them, you're either closing in on your skeleton or are swollen, unrecognizable from the steroids. When the pain gets bad, they start you on oxycodone, but it stops working at some point, and they bring out the big guns, and on those days, you see your friends hovering outside the window and you wonder if you can fly, too.

I was rarely alone unless I asked to be, and as the medicine cocktail drained me of my strength and youth, it also chased away old wounds. My mother and sister rotated at my bedside, watching hours of tennis and junk television. And while it was all too much for my father, I felt no animosity for his inability to sit the same long hours they did. I would need him in time, and we would mend our fences then.

From my hospital bed, I was forced to unwind business and relationships that, in another life, might have ended differently. Something Corporate was put on a more definite hiatus. If cancer does one thing, it reminds you that time is fleeting, and I began prioritizing how I would spend mine if I made it back to the world. My heart was in Jack's Mannequin, and rather than leave my old bandmates hanging on, I had hoped they would leverage what we built into dreams they could maintain without me. At the same time, a series of small flings from my brief stint as a bachelor were extinguished with short phone calls or messages left unreturned. With energy in short supply, you learn to pick your battles or to avoid them altogether.

For all the talk of fighting, I was acclimating to the concept of surrender. Days when everything hurt, I would meditate, and the pain would subside. At first it was counterintuitive—the body wants to meet the enemy with force—but the enemy is within, and the medicine works better when you rest. So I sought peace in that hospital room. Kate brought in yogis and healers to help me breathe, and using what I learned from them, I was able to manage and often transcend my pain. The mind is powerful, and when you're at the edge, it is capable of miraculous things. I relaxed and let my body host the war. My mother took leave from the hotel and spent her days at my bedside; Kelly took the afternoons and the nights, and we lay together making plans for a future that might never come. All the while, I willed the toxic water to do its worst, believing if I stayed still and let it, I might one day climb from the wreckage of me.

To kill the cancer, you kill yourself and pray for revival at the altar of science and your will to survive. Once the chemo brings you to your knees, you wait. If you are lucky, your blood counts recover and you can be in the world without fear of the wind blowing, but it's the moments when there is nothing left to protect you when you have the most to fear. Pneumonia would be my body's first test.

My condition had been deteriorating for days. The doctors did everything they could to treat the cough, but it turned on me, and things fell apart quickly after that. The calm of recent weeks gave way to desperation and bartering with God. I entered and exited consciousness in a room full of people from morning to night with my lungs drowning and my fever so high they kept my body packed on ice. For three nights I hunted oxygen in the dark while my family waited for a signal from the nurses to say goodbye.

Kelly had gone to San Diego for a job interview the morning before my fever spiked. She spent a rare night at home and then returned the following evening. By the time she arrived my condition had become dire; no one had called her, she had been kept in the dark. While she would guard her anger for years, my family's choice not to tell her how close I was to the end would forever alter her trust in them. When

I regained consciousness, she was at my bedside, working cold cloths against my paper skin. The white cells I'd been waiting for arrived just in time. My blood had found a way. Six weeks of beatings had left me unrecognizable, but the staff wrote my walking papers just the same. I'd survived my first round of chemo; the pneumonia landed an early and monumental blow, but I was going home.

Chapter 27

The Junk of Blood and Healing

I'm sorry if the sight of me alarmed you, if you thought you'd seen a ghost. Some days I felt the same just looking in the mirror. My spaceman year was over, our punk rock days were done. I had written my way out thanks to all your cracked teeth and bruises, but it was hard to know what the future held for us. Sitting with you on that first night at home, I dreamed of car speakers and kids with their windows down, and I prayed our songs would find them as wild as I had been when they were written.

♫

The townhouse had been my sanctuary, proof I had made something of myself, and returning to it on the heels of such dangerous days felt like winning. Trejo and Daniels were cautious at first. I couldn't blame them. For years I'd been unstoppable. I felt guilty confronting them with the reality of me, for challenging the notion of what it meant to be young, but they didn't begrudge me my frailty, and their company was a welcome distraction. They had girlfriends now, and it would have been easy for them to hide out in their bedrooms, but we became a family in that house I built for friends.

My days as a one-man army had come to an end. I had closed doors on my past and the people I shared it with, believing I could pave over the ruins if I just kept moving through the dark. But the lights were on now, and the family I had shut out wasn't about to let me slip away. I wondered sometimes if all the junk I'd buried in my blood hadn't come back to haunt me. When you're sick and the doctors can't tell you why, you start trying to answer that question for yourself. Maybe history and family were the poison in my veins, but in the end, they would also be my salvation.

During my stay in the hospital, Dr. Schiller ran labs on all my siblings, and when Kate's, against all odds, revealed our marrows were perfectly matched, he pitched an unconventional course of action: a stem cell transplant. The conversation went something like this: "If it works, I believe she's your best chance at a cure; if it doesn't, we've exhausted our moonshot early and there will be little more I can do for you." My sister and I were raised in a house on fire; we got out with our lives, but the memories were like fires of their own. Kate grew up to find black days and demons of unimaginable prowess, and I grew up to find myself devoured by a cancer of the blood. Fate had now placed us in the arena together—Kate with her strength coming back and me, stripped of everything. She fought her demons first and won, and in agreeing to be my donor, she stepped in to help me fight mine.

I was hellbent on the transplant. The odds of a match had been too slim, and the potential upside too great, to move in any other direction. With my mind made up, Dr. Schiller insisted I come to Los Angeles and meet with him. My mother drove me to the appointment. So much of the life we had shared up to that point was forged inside a moving car, but with the exception of our drive from Ohio, no other had been more consequential than the one we made that afternoon. In the months to come we'd spend hours together traveling in traffic to have my blood drawn from a port installed in my right forearm. The same arm I tattooed for my uncle Stuart. Every dose of chemo, every transfusion, painkiller, and bag of liquid antibiotics up to that point had passed directly through the words he imparted to me from a hospital bed of his own: "Be Positive." Those days my mom liked to say I was finishing the fight my uncle couldn't. I'm not sure it was true, but who could blame her, hunting for a little justice.

We waited outside Dr. Schiller's office not knowing what was in store for us. I had come to care for him during my first hospital stay. His initial stoicism revealed itself in time to be guarding a cautious comedian, one who kept me at arm's length but, I could tell, was so wholly invested in my survival. The more we got to know each other, the more often he trashed my music from his classical high horse, and when his daily rounds coincided with visits from yogis or healers, he took pleasure in drawing distinctions between his work and theirs. I appreciated the bravado, and he played his part well, but his ridicule was always accompanied by a subtle nod. He knew how committed I was, and I trusted him completely. But when he invited my mother and me into his office that Friday afternoon, there was nothing funny about our exchange. The decision I was making would be the biggest of my life, and he spent the hour framing it in the cold concrete of science and fact.

One by one, he pummeled us with odds and side effects. He dragged my mother and I into the deep earth of tragic outcomes, and when he dismissed us, we retired to the hallway in shock. Sitting beside her, in a pale blue corridor, I didn't see the fragile woman on the patio with her ashtray and her cigarettes. I saw the friend who took me on my first road trip and sang along to Bon Jovi for a thousand miles—not because she liked it but because I did. I saw the mother who saved my piano and kept us fed when my father couldn't, and the woman who dressed up for dinner parties and drove me to auditions. And then I saw her hanging upside down from a seatbelt on a highway in the rain, just after our car came to a stop, me wondering at sixteen if I had killed her in that crash. In me, I saw the boy I'd been, before the music and the staircase in Ohio, before the relapses, record deals, and bands imploding in hotel rooms. What is it about the chemistry of sickness and a mother's love? We return to the ones who carried us when we can no longer carry ourselves, our histories erased, and our scores settled. Perhaps not forever, but for a time. And then, beneath the weight of too much truth, I reached for her and she caught me, her resolve without cracks, her body like a life raft.

Chapter 28

The
Jungle

I wrote my first will a month before my twenty-third birthday. A document designed to keep my loved ones from fighting if the cancer claimed me. Arvis would be in charge of unwinding my business. The proceeds from my catalog and the sale of my house would be split between my family and Kelly, and what little I owned after that would be divided among my roommates and friends. I was to be cremated—my funeral would be a concert, no clergy involved or ceremonies in houses of worship. The instructions I mapped out in black ink and capital letters took up less than a page of yellow legal paper. I sealed them in an envelope with an inscription—"Because you've gotta stop rockin' sometime." It was a corny line, but I hoped that it would make Kelly smile if she was forced to read the contents it contained. Years later, I would come across that envelope in a bedside drawer, and the sight of it would resurrect the memory of those days inside my body. For years it would be like this. Some minor souvenir could drag me, unwilling, back to the fevers and trembling legs, back to the once-solid earth crumbling.

Kelly stayed with me at the townhouse most nights, and when the sleeping pills didn't work, we talked about dying. The fear of death visited mostly in the dark hours when the house was still. We would lie there with our unanswered questions, waiting for the moment to pass and for sleep to come. I had remanded control by then, my body and my situation proof enough I had little to begin with, and while there were moments of terror, they were brief and did little to rob me of the calm I wore like a second skin. There was a rhythm to those days: weekly checkups, dinners at my parents' house, nurses dropping by with IV antibiotics, and friends smoking weed while heckling George Bush from the living room sofa. It almost felt normal.

While I gathered strength and waited for the pneumonia to clear, Kate got daily shots to stimulate her white blood and bone marrow in preparation for the transplant. The process lasted two weeks, left her exhausted, and when it was complete, they stuck an IV in one arm, drew her blood into a centrifuge, and then fed it back into her body through an IV in the other. Her extracted stem cells would be frozen and then transfused through a port in my chest once I had been sufficiently destroyed by the chemo and radiation. In the days leading up to the harvest, I returned to Fourth Street for the first time in months. It was a stark reminder of how truly far I had traveled in a short time. My voice was small and my body ached behind the keys of the piano. No one said it out loud, but those of us gathered for the session knew it might be my last. Nevertheless, the song I recorded that day was not intended for the world, but instead for an audience of one: my marrow twin sister, Kate.

It was the fifteenth of August when I moved back to UCLA, and knowing what I did of passing time in hospital rooms, I made the place my own. I covered the walls in Polaroids and posters, installed lamps and a Japanese fountain. Morning would signal the assault: four days of radiation to my brain and body followed by four days of chemo and the transplant. My blood would begin its familiar descent, and when the counts reached zero, rather than willing my immune system to return, we would be rooting for my sister's instead. What could go wrong?

I was living my life at the intersection of faith and science. Not the faith I lost in confirmation classes, latched to the good book and a God with a son. This was my faith in the thread and the cell. The Holy connector that I had come to believe bound everything to everyone. The music that in some ways had delivered me to that bed and that fight was a testament to following signs. And in one final signal from the gods or whatever, *Everything in Transit*, the album of songs I had given up so much to create, was scheduled to be released on the same day as the transplant that would be my eventual cure.

August 23, 2005: The Transplant

The day began with a visit from a healer who believed that I suffered from a broken heart. After my year of breakups with the band and with Kelly, it was easy to believe, but she saw something deeper, something it would take me years to understand. I had been shaped in the shadow of my family tree. I had learned to run, and I would keep running until I sought out my past with an eye on forgiveness. If only I had seen it then, but I didn't. I believed my parents' acts of love and sacrifice in that moment would be enough to redeem all our history for good, but I would survive those hospital days, and everything I had kept locked up would meet me on the other side. Only then, I would be compromised, twisted into a complex knot of fear, confusion, gratitude, and guilt for living—an orgy of trauma I would be too proud to confront and too lost to unwind. I couldn't fix what I couldn't see though, and the morning I received Kate's cells, it didn't matter. Forgiveness isn't always absolute, and while mine turned out to be conditional, in that moment, all I felt for my family was love.

They gathered at my bedside, and we watched the marrow travel through a PICC line in my chest, willing its safe passage, but stopping short of predicting the future. When it was over, we sat, hands held in silent knowledge of the siege. My skin, browning from the radiation, lent cover to the wilderness it contained, but everyone in the room knew what was happening: warring factions, blood against blood. Both would need to forge treaties if I was to survive. I worried for Kate. Would she blame herself if it wasn't enough? I was certain she would.

Weeks passed in the jungle of my conception. I was the host now; my insides twitched, and everything was dangerous. The rashes began; my mouth and throat became a cave and a runway on fire. I turned twenty-three with my skin peeling and body shuddering outside my control. In another world, I would have spent the week supporting my album's release, making the rounds to press, late-night television, and record stores—but in this one, a formidable army of label staff and die-hard fans had run up the numbers in my absence. The album charted without me there to do the work. I was grateful, but, for the first time in my life, music was no longer my concern.

With Labor Day came a break in the violence. Kelly and I spent the long weekend entwined, and at night she retired to a cot at my bedside where we would sleep with our hands held like a bridge between the elevations. A welcome vacation until the blister arrived. It started as a boil on my ribcage, lighting up nerve paths with razorblade fireworks, and in the days that followed, it matured into a black scab wrapping the entirety of my torso's right half. Shingles. Never have I known such pain. My new immune system was unprepared for the early, heavy lift, and the virus, unchecked, conquered me. I cycled through pain meds until I reached the morphine mountain top where I lay, hallucinating for days. But unlike the pneumonia, this was not a thing sent to kill me, and despite its brutality and theft of my will, my bedridden body had started making good blood again.

I returned to my parents' house on the twelfth of September. I remember the car ride at night and being carried through the door. There was no celebration, no welcome party; I was too far gone for company and balloons. The first night passed with my parents and Kelly at my bedside, their hands on my limbs until the morning, when my eyes finally closed. The days that followed were molasses and fire, passing in snapshots between labored eye openings and human crutch carries to the bathroom. When Kelly couldn't spend the night, my parents took shifts to keep me from sleepwalking and falling downstairs.

At home, after the transplant, it fell on my mother and father to manage my pain. There were pages of instructions and enough orange pill bottles to line a wall in the corner of the kitchen. There were antibiotics, steroids, anti-rejection meds, and pain pills, each with their own finely printed marching orders and dosages not to exceed. My parents followed all the rules, but the shingles were like knives all over, and when it came to the pain medication, administering the daily limit was enough to extinguish the light in me. What a choice—agony or oblivion.

I was prewired for addiction, and in the days leading up to the hospital and New York, I felt myself caving to its gravitational pull. Whether I would have given in or not I'll never know, but I *was* out of control, and winding up sidelined, I felt relieved—like the universe had conspired to protect me from myself. Ironically though, it was not the parties or self-medicating that landed me briefly in the arms of addiction, it was the hospital, the morphine drip and the black scab that followed me home. When I returned to Dr. Schiller's clinic weeks later for a checkup, pill numb and keeling, he canceled my prescriptions on the spot. I can only imagine the shame my parents felt when he told them he hadn't saved my life so I could waste it as a junkie. It wasn't their fault I had gotten hooked, but it would be their burden to unhook me.

I came back from that appointment with all the pain and no medicine—so my father stepped in, moving me down the hall into the bedroom he shared with my mother, tending to me around the clock. Had he been there before, in that very same bed, twitching in a cold sweat, crawling to the bathroom to retch with his cheek on the porcelain, too tired for a little dignity? I suspected he had, and it was his aim to ensure I didn't go through it alone. For all we had been through, I still loved him. Through his relapses and lost jobs, he had kept his hope alive, and in those slow hours the gift of his quiet assurance helped me do the same.

For days, he orbited with a clairvoyant awareness of what came next and how to make it hurt less. Ice packs, blankets, shades drawn, hands on, hands off, water, and a little food. He had been no stranger in my hospital room but deferred to the women who were stronger than he was and better suited for my care. But in the blackest hours of my pain and purging, it was he who carried me through, our strange roads merging, if only briefly, to bless me with the gift of his uncompromised presence and him with the gift of being needed. It always struck me as tragic, how much he lost and how visibly he carried his shame, but if those days taught me anything, it is that our tragic lessons are lessons, nonetheless.

Detoxed, the fog relented, and I took stock of my body in the mirror. I was 114 pounds, my skin was taut, cracking in places and oozing in others. My lips were white with dry craters and my feet were so plagued by neuropathy that I would teach myself to walk again without feeling them. There wasn't a dusting of hair across my alien frame, and my bones were so free of meat and muscle that I dressed for winter in the warmth of the sun. This was the fallout, the ground zero of me, and to know it was to find hope and start rebuilding.

By the middle of October my condition was stable, and I returned to the townhouse once more. It had been the longest summer I had known. Things moved slowly at first. The anti-rejection medicine was unpredictable, making it hard to leave the house, but I learned to work around it and eventually made my way back into the world. I couldn't watch the news without weeping or step outside without kissing the ground. My exhaustion and gratitude were bound to each other like a breath cycle: inhale, exhale, life at the marathon finish line. But my life was not over—it was beginning anew, and with my energy returning so was my ambition.

If you're lucky, you're back on your feet within a year of a transplant, but I refused to accept the timeline. My label and management brought me opportunities, and I fell into the old habit of saying yes when I should have said no. I recorded at Fourth Street, gave interviews, and in December, on the one-hundred-day anniversary of my transplant, I played a free show for a room full of people who had refused to give up on me. Jacques had moved on by then, but with Jim and the remaining members of Jack's Mannequin at my side, I played a set tailored to my voice, which was still healing. Later that month, I took Kelly out to dinner in San Diego and asked her to be my wife. I was ready for the hard days to be over.

Chapter 29

OUR HOUSE
IN THE TREES

Kelly and I were married on December 16, 2006. I had spent the months leading up to the wedding on the road, surrounded by party friends, pretending the cancer hadn't changed me when I knew it had. I went roller-skating on ecstasy, took the last of my meds onstage with a shot of Jägermeister, and, in a signal of what was to come, I showed up to my one-year transplant checkup drunk with my clothes soaked in minibar liquor. I had become a walking "fuck you" to the thing I had survived, daring it to come back and kill me. But for all my running and denial, Kelly held on to her faith in me.

I sold the townhouse I shared with Trejo and Daniels and started over in Los Angeles, in a hideout at the top of Mulholland Drive—a treehouse with a view from every window. Arvis retired from the road, went to work for my manager, and for the next five years lived with Kelly and me as we rode out the aftermath of my disease. As insane as it all sounds, those bender days felt more like a celebration than a prelude to a darker time, and I suppose if they had ended sooner, they might have been. No one hands you a map at the hospital door calling out the traps in your path, and even if they had, I probably would have been too cavalier to take one. I had stepped back into the world, and though it looked just like I had remembered it, everything was temporary now. "You're better," they said, and "it's time to move on." So Kelly and I moved on. Or, at least, we tried.

It's hard to look back now and separate the desperation from the relief, the alienation from the triumph, the gratitude from the mourning. But I was alive, I was still young, and though I was stepping into strange days, I had held on to my love and my music. And on the night of our wedding, as I watched Kelly walk down the aisle to the sound of Etta James with a light rain falling on the roof above us, I couldn't help but sing along, "At last." Whatever we had been through, the site of her in that white dress was proof we had survived it together. The ceremony was short, and we laughed at the part about sickness and health, and then we said, "I do." We were kids, forging ahead in the aftermath of a hurricane, with our parents in the front row, biting their tongues. Maybe we weren't ready, but the day was earned, no matter what the future had in store for us. And when I delivered my toast, I saw Dr. Schiller and his wife sitting at a table with my friends, and I raised a glass to him and a day that very well may never have come.

When it was all over, Kelly and I spent the weekend in a hotel bed. I remember waking up the morning after the wedding and drinking Champagne on the balcony together. I took a picture of our bare feet resting on a railing side by side, and, in a rare moment, the peace I had felt in the hospital returned to me. I didn't miss being sick, but I missed the clarity I had encountered pressed up against the boundary of life. I kept the picture and the memory of that balcony close in the coming years, caught between my desire to move beyond the cancer and my clinging to the past it interrupted. Kelly and I had no idea what was coming for us, and in a way I'm glad we didn't, because we had fought to wear those rings, to drink that Champagne, and to return to our little treehouse, married.

When the weekend was over, we drove back to Los Angeles and closed out our year in the hills. Our time in the house on Mulholland was short-lived and legendary. We had no television there or drapes on the windows, which wrapped around three sides of the top floor. At night, the traffic and city lights from Downtown to Venice became a blanket of earthbound stars. Our bedroom faced east, where counting sunrises was worth the intrusion, and on one perfect morning Kelly and I made love with "Hallelujah" playing on repeat. When I wasn't on the road, friends and eccentrics—my sister Kate and my parents among them—traversed the hillside, joining us for nights that stretched into the morning. The proximity of my fighting days cast those gatherings as celebrations at the end of the world or perhaps at the beginning. Survivorship and the wagon train of baggage it came with would soon be laid bare, but for a moment, things were perfect.

I remember it was hot that night. For a year we lived in those trees. You had a room on the first floor with white walls and a blue tweed couch that cost more than the rent. I dragged us both up that hill, looking for a place to hide. Somewhere my hospital year wouldn't hold its sway over us. The night before we moved out, I wandered down the stairs to say goodbye to you. The songs we had written afforded me a fresh start in a new home on another hill, one I probably could have seen from the balcony of that treehouse through a pair of good binoculars, though I never tried. The new place had room for a baby grand and windows facing west. Four years of sunsets ahead. I didn't want to let you go, but there's something that happens when you get sick so young. You start looking back at life before the hammer dropped: a life of abandon, wonder, and fearlessness. That life is gone. I couldn't bear to look at you most days; every sticker on your skin, a reminder I had become somebody new. Someone more cautious. Less free. It wasn't your fault, but the melodies and forms, the words and reinvention you bore witness to, had become too much to confront. In all my years of writing and living on the other side of eighty-eight teeth, I never thought to call my pianos what they were. Friends. The most willing companions. And you were my best friend. Yes, we fought, and so many days I beat my head against your frame, begging for a lightning strike. That night though, I saw you for what you were: the keeper of my secrets, the arbiter of my voice. So selfless, you asked nothing of me, and I demanded everything from you. How cruel I was, shipping you off to that dark valley closet to collect dust. I knew you would forgive me, but it would take me time to forgive myself—for letting you go, for losing sight of so much that mattered in the fog of my recovery. Still, our last night in your little room on Mulholland was magic. The dance of creation, perfect for the first time since the cancer. The weaving of the words, the arch of the melody, the form so seemingly simple yet deceptively complex. They all just arrived as if channeled from some other world. Rain on the windowsill one moment, sunshine through the clouds the next. You blink and there it is . . . the song.

♫

Piano Three

Reborn, the Organic Machine

The piano is not unlike a human, with its
most impressive features sometimes doubling
as its fatal flaws. On a stage alone, in a
finely tuned hall, the piano can reach an audience
of thousands without the use of a single
microphone. Its wooden belly is an amplifier so
remarkable that all it gathers—both within it
and without—will be cast into the world as sound.
But the sad fact of this brilliant design
leaves the piano in a perilous condition when
sharing space with other noisemakers.
Within earshot of a drum set or electric
amplification, the music played on a piano

can be compromised, even buried. Solving for this problem leads us to the most recent and often frowned-on evolution of the acoustic piano: the incorporation of electronic systems.

For stages where microphones alone won't do the trick, acoustic pianos may be modified to provide the player and the audience with a lifelike experience—one that, decades ago, would have been impossible to deliver. And while the purity of the piano's live sound may be supplemented or replaced entirely by the samples it generates, for a player who might otherwise be stuck behind the plastic keys of a synthesizer, these advances are, without question, a gift.

Chapter 30

BULLETPROOF
Frankenstein

I pulled you from a showroom floor and had a matching model sent to live with me in Silverlake at the hill house near the reservoir. Baby grands, identical but for your skins. I had lived my life reflected in the black satin mirrors of my first two pianos and chose your matte mahogany finish knowing I'd never meet my gaze within it. You took the stage light like a mansion heirloom, but you rode the highways with me: two hundred sleepless nights a year, your eighty-eight cat- apults working under pressure. Your closed lid became my perch, a stage within a stage, and I ascended my throne to your platform nightly to marvel at the human moving seas. It didn't take long to realize you were more trouble than I bargained for, but by then I had become a magnet for resistance. There were nights I drank too much onstage and woke up to your whiskey-stuck keys, and there were shows that ended with your pedal box and lyre ripped loose under the pressure of my lead foot sustain. Your legs trembled, your roof flexed and bowed, and by the end of your first year, you had a hardware store's worth of new glue and screws on board. When talk of your early retirement was raised, we devised a plan, a surgery that would have horrified your maker. When you returned, your wooden legs had been replaced by paint-matched, powder-coated steel, and your lyre, your pedal box, and backstays had been outfitted with a metal housing to keep them from ripping off midshow. I was a mess and took the fight to you, nightly, but you were ready…my bulletproof Frankenstein.

♫

Chapter 31

The Family
You
Choose

I returned to the world of color and noise rebranded a hero. I was not. Given the choice to fight or die, most everybody fights—but the press loves a comeback kid, and I played the part. The attention was flattering at first, but as the distance grew between the person I was and the person I was perceived to be, I rebelled, chasing denial and post-traumatic stress through a maze of blackouts and broken glass. When I think about those days, those years really…the aftermath, it's easy to get lost in the dark. And while I could fill pages with the mistakes I made, my resurrection as a rock star and manic cannonball was a whole lot of fun…until it wasn't.

Raw, JayMac, and Jon were family now, and our home was the road and Los Angeles. Like brothers, they stood by me, even when my uncertain future called theirs into question. And though we had been a good band before my blood-sick detour, we were indomitable upon my return, playing with a vengeance for that stolen year. From showtime to the black-and-blue dawn the world was ours, and we spun through it—a joyful cataclysm—passing bottles, playing DJ in the front lounge of the bus, and folding the sick into their beds, with trash bags taped to the sides of their faces, hoping to spare the hallway of a late-night purge.

At home our circle had expanded. Kelly found sisters in Jen and Jessie, JayMac's and Raw's future wives. They kept each other upright for years—three unlikely companions, all their grit boxed up in beauty, all their loyalty asleep in beds alone. While the band and I traveled, the three of them convened after work and on the weekends; though we were miles apart, the six of us looked in on one another, three clustered families, intimate by proxy, no man or woman left behind.

When a tour ended, the band and I would bring the circus home with us, throwing parties and closing down bars, and with Arvis living down the hall from Kelly and me and most of our crew within minutes, we took to swinging from the rafters, nightly. There was beauty in our wild ways, but I stop short of nostalgia, knowing my party crown was fixed to a mask. Privately, I was buried. Depressed without naming it. I was a changed man in a world that had moved on without me. Like I said, it was a whole lot of fun until it wasn't.

By the summer of '07, pressure was mounting for the follow-up album I had been compiling in fits and starts. Compared with the age of abandon that inspired its predecessor, *Everything in Transit,* my new life felt remote, hemmed in. I was bulletproof with a bar tab and a crowd, but there was no pretending in the studio or the rooms where I wrote. The writer's block was paralyzing at times, and my confidence a fickle wave—it swelled, pitched, and then shattered magnificently before returning to a paper-flat sea. I was beholden to that wave, rushing to the studio and rallying the band when I caught glimpses of the writer I had been.

At fifteen, in the wake of my father's relapse, I sought comfort in control: control of my affections, my money, music, and the destiny I willed into being. I wanted immunity from the impact of the outside world and learned to push people away if they got too close or threatened my ability to move with speed in any chosen direction. It's so obvious to me now—my drifting from Something Corporate, my breakup with Kelly, both were born out of that reflex. I needed too much from them, and I had learned that needing people could be dangerous. So I enacted my will, ran lean, and started over as an island. But cancer quickly foiled my plans for autonomy, and it proved that I could be made helpless, no matter whom I leaned on or sent packing for fear they knew me too well.

For a time, when I was sick, I found comfort in those who watched over me. It felt good to need people again and to feel safe in their care. But as the months and years collected in the wake of my illness, once again, I made targets of those closest to me. By then, my fearlessness was gone. I could not evade what I learned as a sick man, or the gnawing uncertainty that disease had unleashed into my once-sacred spaces. I became a beggar for my songs, for my talent and convictions, and my life aboveground. And it was in *those* days that I truly understood what it meant to lose control. So I waited for the wave of my confidence to build and break, jaw locked with little patience. The momentum and certainty that had steered me through my life and music was hard to come by, and it stretched the making of my album over three calendar years.

My aimlessness and inability to focus were not without consequence. When it came to the band, I relied on their time and talents but refused them equity or a seat at the table. Too blind to do the business right, my failure to fully include them watered seeds of grievance. In Arvis, I had a friend and trusted adviser, and I repaid his loyalty with tirades and paranoia. He had spent years cleaning up my messes, but his days as my psychedelic chaperone had yielded to the management of my fists and their directionless swinging.

No one suffered more than Kelly. The harder it was for me to write, the more impossible I was to be around. I made a criminal of her, blamed her when the music didn't come to me, and waxed nostalgic for the days I lived alone. We were known for nights with catastrophic ends. Dark bars and dance floors where we spent the early hours wrapped up in each other could turn volatile around closing time. I was dangerous with a drink in my hand, leaping from affection to resentment, from reverie to the bottom of a well. Kelly had learned how to handle me in the daylight—but in the bars, one wrong turn and we would be swept up into the corners, separated by friends or thrown into cabs before paying the bill. All to keep the scene from boiling over. Show me a fuse, and I'll show you a man who likes playing with fire. It could be anything: jealousy, politics, or the weather. Kelly gave the signal and I'd strike the match, and we would launch fireworks into the morning.

Still, those days were never just one thing. For all the anger, there was joy, and for all the wandering, there was purpose. The cold clouds of hopelessness would swell inside our home, then some word I had scribbled in a dream would find me in the morning, and a song would temporarily cast them out. There were nights we fought, and there were mornings we woke up just to watch the sunrise. And though I was in no place to captain the massive undertakings of my marriage, art, and business, each reflected the bedlam and the faith of those up-and-down days. And there is beauty in that, I suppose.

By the end of '07, I was finding my way in the studio, though it was hard to tell the difference between a lifeboat and a song. In lieu of the counseling I should have sought for my troubled reentry, I focused on the album instead, believing that the music would help me make sense of my life after cancer. My timing couldn't have been worse. The record business was in decline—the labels had ignored the warning signs, attempting to rein in piracy rather than evolve—and the climate of fear and consolidation made it difficult to get the budget for my album approved. At the time, my creativity was fragile, my output sporadic, and rather than wait for permission from the label, I recorded when I felt inspired, writing checks out of my own bank account.

By January my debt had ballooned—the label refused to pay its bills, and I was forced to shut down production of the album.

How either of us survived those first few years is beyond me—you, with your metal legs, and me with my sabotage. The schedule alone should have broken us both. When the touring burnout set in, we would come home and camp out in rented rooms despite my house full of pianos. You spent your nights alone, but I killed the days with you, hoping to return home around dark with a song. We had a ramshackle writing hut on the Eastside, prone to regular power outages and ongoing construction. I wrote a song there in the dark and called it "Caves." After that, I rented us a loft downtown with floor-to-ceiling windows and overpriced gear, installed but never used. The place wasn't cheap, but I wrote a song there called "The Resolution," and its success covered the rent that year. In the end, I pissed a small fortune down the drain paying piano movers so we could pal around like idiots in love, but the people keeping the books those days liked me well-fed and uninformed, and cut the checks to keep us traveling freely.

♫

Chapter 32

The Glass Passenger

I get restless easily, and by January of '08 if I wasn't moving, I was consumed. Some would call it depression, but for me it was a house guest, a spirit arriving without invitation and departing without notice. I never heard the door crack when it entered, but I knew it was there when the morning came, and my body felt like concrete in bed. I would smoke weed all day and drink in the bars at night, tending to the intruder who only seemed to leave when a song made its way through me and into the world. So I spent the months before Christmas 2007 working, staring at the keys of my piano until the writer's block cleared, and moving quickly to the studio once it had. The label was probably right to be worried. I wasn't watching the bottom line—I was hanging on for dear life. I had been working that way for more than a year, and though it wasn't a cure, focusing on music kept me from going under completely. Then just as I felt my confidence returning, the label intervened. I couldn't afford to do it my way any longer, and without their support, the sessions couldn't continue, and the album was put on hold. With no studio to run to, I was afraid of being home when the house guest called again, so I reached out to Trejo, hoping a change of scenery would keep me in the light.

Day 1—Los Angeles, Las Vegas, and a Phone Call Home

The backpack had a change of clothes, a journal, and a ziplocked baggie full of freshly rolled joints. I threw it in the trunk and held Kelly by the car's half-opened door, my chin resting on her shoulder and my eyes fixed on our home, which rose from the patchwork hills. The house had a green zinc roof and a path of matching emerald slate that connected it to the driveway, where my car was parked, packed and running. That home was the first we owned together, and we bought it from the builder brand new. And though it was more than we needed, we poured ourselves into making it our own. We got a dog and named her Doris Day, bought new furniture, and ordered a vintage door, which I refinished myself; I botched the job but I was proud of my work just the same. The sun was setting as we said our goodbyes, and I knew Kelly would return to find the entryway washed in a shifting pink light. What I *didn't* know was how that house—its rooms, its halls, its windows—would be the backdrop to our years of hope and pain.

With the album stalled, I needed a few days to clear my head. Trejo had moved to Nevada; he had left home and gone searching elsewhere, just like I had. With no music to make and no shows to play, I craved his easy company. Reversing up the sloping drive, I took one final look at Kelly and another at the house we shared, which, like everything those days, seemed to be hanging precariously from a cliff's edge.

Vegas wasn't far. I had made the drive so many times by then I could have done it in my sleep. I had planned to spend a few days in Henderson, Nevada, at Trejo's apartment, writing when he worked, and trolling the casinos together at night. But the farther I traveled from my record and the pressure I was under, the more I craved the alchemy of solitude and motion. Miles of highway with nowhere to be. The need to keep driving felt less like a choice and more like a calling. I decided to abandon my original plan—a short visit with a friend a few hours away—in favor of something more ambitious. A road trip without a destination, without a calendar. A meditation at full speed.

Kelly had grown wary of me; I could hear it again in her voice when I called from the road; I had been driving for less than an hour. She bore the brunt of my roller-coaster moods, the sharp turns of animation and lethargy. Ever since the hospital, I had grown suspicious of the ground beneath me. Certain I would be drawn down into the quicksand of depression or that I would fall through one of cancer's trapdoors, I moved through the world in a zigzag, afraid. Kelly kept up, but I wasn't easy to love, and it took a toll on her. It's not that there weren't bright days, but the dark ones cast long shadows, and when I phoned her halfway to Barstow, with my new plan to drive until I had run out of road, it was the trapdoors and pressure, the coaster and the quicksand, I was running from.

I met Trejo at his restaurant before closing. The Sweetwater had all the trappings of a chain despite being an upstart, a focus-grouped logo in neon and a sizable footprint swallowing its fair share of the strip mall it operated out of. The place was empty when I arrived, but by then, Trejo said it looked the same most hours of the day. His bosses had been counting on a clientele of homeowners from the nearby developments that had sprung up in the recent housing boom. But the global financial crisis was closing in, and the restaurant would eventually implode alongside the neighborhoods it aimed to serve. A theater of war for the outgunned American dream.

Trejo and I found a bar and caught up over cheap beers and video blackjack, and I couldn't help but miss the days we shared a roof, when I had a little more faith in the future. But wherever life was taking us, our friendship came easy, and for the night I wasn't a singer in a band or a cancer survivor—I was the fat kid in the backseat with the windows down, so grateful just to be known.

We stayed out late that night to make up for the time we had missed, avoiding the strip in favor of local dives and half-priced debauchery. Trejo was the captain, I was happy in the passenger seat, and we proceeded through the night, reminiscing, making house calls to his friends, and touring the suburban backbone of a city we had grown up cruising on fake IDs. Vegas had always been Trejo's town, so when he found work nearby, none of us were surprised to see him go. It takes guts to leave home, to start over somewhere new, and even though I had done it my whole life, I never had to do it alone.

We pushed into the morning hours knowing our time would be cut short by my plan to keep moving; we woke up hungover and drove to North Vegas, where I bought a keyboard off a kid on Craigslist. I was hoping to write my way across America.

I didn't.

We stopped for one last beer at the T-Bird Lounge, a jukebox dive with a couple of big screens, a pool table, and smoke so thick you could move it with your hands. Then Trejo got into his car and I got into mine, and with the sun in my eyes I set sail. The loose plan was to cross the country, and with winter bearing down in most of America, the southern route was the obvious choice. I headed southeast out of Henderson and picked up the 40 in Kingman, Arizona.

Day 2—The House of Dreams

I might have stopped to sleep somewhere along the way, but the only thing I recall between Vegas and Albuquerque is the meteor crater in Winslow, Arizona—a fifty-thousand-year-old punch in the crust of the earth about a mile in diameter and nearly six hundred feet deep. A mining family had purchased the rights to the land more than a hundred years before and now sold tickets to people like me who had nothing but time in the middle of nowhere. I got high in the parking lot, paid the entry fee, and climbed into the hollow, thinking about the wife I had left behind. When I called her from the road the previous evening to break the news of my new plan, she had left me rattled with her parting question: "You're not leaving me, are you?" Kelly had swallowed those words for months or more, and they would continue to chase us through the coming years. The answer was no. It was always no, but her suspicion was earned. I had threatened to walk out on her before, mostly when I felt stuck, so desperate to blame her for my captivity. But my jailer was *me*: a man obsessed with a past he couldn't alter. I sat for an hour in that hole in the Arizona desert, a testament to things colliding and shapes forever changed. I felt at home there.

I reached Albuquerque before midnight. The Casa de Suenos was an artists' colony in the first half of the twentieth century; it had since been preserved as a kitsch hotel, and I decided to spend a few days there on the promise of its antiquity and muse. I set up the keyboard in the kitchen of the El Prado Suite, and while it mostly stared me down, I felt inspired there, and that was enough for me. I made day trips to Madrid and Santa Fe, wandered the old town square looking for night life where there was none, and when word reached my old friend Andy that I was in town, we made plans to catch up over drinks. Andy had just moved to Albuquerque, but I knew him as a scene kid from Oklahoma, stick thin and always on fire. In another life, he sold merchandise for my first band, and like so many I've known who sling cloth for a living, he had charisma and a sixth gear.

We spent the night discussing the turns our lives had taken: marriage, God, and disease. Andy found Jesus and followed a pastor's daughter to New Mexico, turning his back on the lifestyle that had been central to so many of our fond, shared memories. Lost Boys leave Neverland sometimes, and I grieved his departure like an abandoned Peter Pan. He seemed happy though, and I did my best to be happy for him. It's easy to burn out on the road—I understood it. I had woken up plenty of mornings in need of salvation, but some part of me believed I would make it through my reckless years, and I was content to wait it out.

We left the bar, and with nothing better to do, we decided to make the two-hour round-trip to Santa Fe, knowing nights like those were precious, and sleep a waste of time. I guess I wasn't the only one craving the road those days. We listened to music and told our stories while the tires turned, and in that sense, some things hadn't changed. Andy dropped me back at the Casa in the dark hours of early morning, and we said our goodbyes. We stayed friends, and every now and again I would run into him at a show. On one occasion, I confessed I was struggling, admitting that I'd spent my fair share of nights with a bottle in a black hole, and he attempted to convert me on the spot. I passed. Andy had his church and I had mine. In the end, he would forgive me for sticking it out as a heathen, and I'd forgive him for growing up.

Day 5—Baptized on the Interstate

I had been crisscrossing the country in buses and vans for years, but never had I driven the length of Texas alone. Millions of acres of valleys, deserts, and hill country stretched out beneath a sky so wide and prone to cloud mountains. I quit the 40 before leaving New Mexico, ate lunch in Lubbock, laid flowers at the grave of Buddy Holly, and caught a speeding ticket on my way out of town. With half the country behind me, I shut off my phone, disappeared into the panorama, and found what I'd been missing all along: the space between breaths, the sense of destiny I had lost after the hospital, my faith in the music I was making, and the smallness of me inside the cradle of something much bigger. Back then I couldn't admit to anyone how destroyed I was by the cancer, and in my denial, I became a secret to the world. I had been so fortunate to survive and wore my gratitude like a mask in public, ashamed of the wounds it concealed. But alone on that road I found forgiveness, for myself and for the days that changed me. It was a private baptism, one that wouldn't last in the real world, but for a moment I made contact with the peace I had been seeking.

I have no record of where I went from there, no letters or journal entries to explain the time I lost, just the memory of floating, my car, a speck of dust on one of earth's perfect landscapes, dressed in the changing colors of the day. Did the sun set and my mood shift as darkness claimed the road? Did I pull off for some food and a bed with clean sheets? Maybe I stayed in Abilene, because I liked the way it sounded, and then slept through the night for the first time in years. Maybe it was Wichita Falls or Shreveport, Little Rock or Texarkana. Wherever I landed, I'm sure I was dreaming of New Orleans, but driving farther south had implications for my soul, so I kept moving east with my eyes on the finish.

Day 7—A Night in Tennessee

When I came to, the big skies were behind me, and I could feel January through the window on the back of my hand. I was barreling down the 40 to Nashville and called Carl from the road on my approach. Carl was my manager; we had worked together for nearly six years. He was a born hustler in horn-rimmed glasses, and though he dealt mostly aboveboard, I'm sure he was no stranger to a backroom deal. By the time I arrived at his doorstep that night, Carl had seen me through a lot. When I was diagnosed in New York City and a private plane was the only safe way home, he made the arrangements and helped foot the bill. When my cancer year put the band out of work, he found them a steady gig, and when Arvis was ready to retire from the road, Carl gave him a desk and a salary. And despite having lost my way, in the studio and in life, I never once questioned Carl's belief in me.

I pulled into the driveway of his sprawling estate, a week deep on two changes of clothes. I had clocked a couple of thousand miles by then, in pursuit of what, I wasn't sure. Carl loved it—my willingness to set fires and run. He was impulsive like me and no stranger to a change in direction. We caught up in the kitchen, whispering to avoid waking his family, and then retired to a screening room to take stock of the music I had been forced to leave behind.

The songs weren't finished, but they were close. Getting them to a point where I felt safe to share them had been painful. I had become obsessive, layering sounds and deconstructing finished work for fear I had missed something essential along the way. Clumsy as I was, I fought for that music and for the illusion of its effortless construction. I pulled a joint from my jacket pocket, and with Carl at my side, we wandered stoned into the wilderness of the thing I had made. It was a document of weirdness and hope, a collection of "blackbox" songs from the crash I had survived, and I was hearing it clearly for the first time. The music wandered in places, but so had I. It soared in others, urging the listener to persist through darkness—I was speaking to myself. And in the end, those songs seemed to beckon me down the very road I was traveling, offering up an empathy I hadn't yet offered myself. I didn't plan to stop in Nashville, I hadn't planned on anything, but sitting there, cracked open and proud of the sounds in those speakers, it seemed I had found another reason for the drive.

I didn't need a map to know where I was going next. Though they had relocated to the West Coast, all three of my bandmates had once called Richmond, Virginia, home, and with our beloved crew member Sorvino living there, the "river city" seemed like a good place to complete my journey. Little did I know a phone call would come the following day and upend my plans once more.

Day 8—The Road to Richmond, We're Only Getting Farther Away

I was halfway to Virginia when the phone rang. It was Manhead, the friend and New Jersey surf-rat who had been printing my T-shirts since the early days. He reminded me of the stoners I grew up with—we traded "dudes" and "mans" and all the accordion slang you earn as a child of the water. We didn't speak often, but every few weeks we'd dig into some epic question, avoiding whatever it was we were meant to be doing at the time. My travels were the topic of the day, and they conjured the wanderlust in him. His friends were getting older and bailing on the trips they used to take. It was freezing in New York, where he lived now, and he was craving the surf in Costa Rica. I was about to run

out of road and saw an opening for both for us. I told him to book a
ticket and I would meet him there.

I had been away from home for more than a week, and though I
checked in along the way, lending assurances of my return, my road
trip woke a fear in Kelly that I might leave her stranded. It had only
been a few years since our breakup, and even closer were the days when
my survival was in question. My impermanence was not abstract. For
Kelly, it was her daily reality.

I knew I was pushing it, but I made the call anyway, revealing my
plans to meet Manhead in Costa Rica. Kelly was silent at first, then
fired on me, heartsick and defiant. Why was I allowed to leave our life
and travel on some open-ended ticket? How was it that all her dreams
had taken a backseat to mine? She was right. She had forfeited a job
offer and a new life on the East Coast to see me through my cancer year.
Then I married her, moved us to Los Angeles, and left her marooned in
the hills while I spent most of my days on tour. Our relationship had
once been so equitable, but the roles changed, with her helping me in
and out of beds and bathtubs, shaving my head and holding cold cloths
to my skin until the fevers broke. I couldn't answer her questions, but
I asked her one in hopes of cushioning the blow. If she could go anywhere, where would it be? She was everyone's rock, a middle child who
had ceded impulsivity to her siblings. But in the end, even she craved
her own disappearing act.

So many of our days together, after the cancer, I had lost sight of
her. I couldn't bring myself to confront her fears, her worry, and her
pain, knowing I'd be forced to confront my own. But I could feel her on
that phone call, the depth of the sadness she had concealed. So much of
it I could have spared her. She deserved more than what I was offering,
but I was too buried in myself to offer much to anyone those days. In
the end, it was Paris she had been dreaming of. I had my trip, and now
she would have hers. She found a little hotel close to the Metro in the
heart of the city, and I went to work booking her travel. She packed

a small bag and was on a plane the next day. Why I didn't cancel my plans and fly to meet her there instead is beyond me, but there's a lot about that time in our lives I'll never understand.

The End of the Road

It had been dark for hours when I finally pulled into Richmond and the Inn at Patrick Henry's, but I wasn't looking for a room, I was looking for Sorvino. He and Raw were best friends, and prior to joining Something Corporate, it was Sorvino's floor that Raw had camped out on to avoid paying rent between tours. Sorv was stout, durable, eternally merry and had been traveling with Jack's Mannequin for a year, tuning guitars and looking after my piano. When he was off the road, he held on to his bartending gig, and I was glad to find him working that night. I descended the stairs to his voice like a kettle drum, the bartender in the basement, my friend, greeting me with a loud and lengthy "PLAYER!" Everyone was a player in Sorv's world. I grabbed a spot at the bar where, for the night, my drinks were free.

It was quiet at the pub, not that most of the stools weren't taken, but compared with the Richmond benders I had grown accustomed to, this was mild fare. The subterranean dive had walls of exposed and painted white brick, and it felt more like a living room from the '70s than a bar. There was a fireplace in the corner and a dark green carpet, and the crown molding connecting the ceiling to the walls was a painted rain gutter masquerading as woodwork. Upstairs was home to a small inn, but the bar itself was a local dive. Raw, JayMac, and Jon had brought me there on our first tour after the hospital. This was before Sorvino joined the crew. He was tending bar that night, and after he closed up, he offered me a ride on the back of his Vespa, which I boarded, and he promptly crashed.

Being in Richmond with the band was like attending a homecoming parade, and by then I had gotten to know most of their friends. They owned restaurants, waited tables, and dealt drugs on the side, and since I had come back to life, we scheduled weekend freak-outs with them every time our bus was in range. I didn't mind the quiet for a change though. I had left my weed in Nashville, experimenting with a little moderation, which felt good. I had made it all the way across the country, and the days of low pressure had tempered my need to be fully submerged. With plans to meet Manhead in Costa Rica in a couple of days, the trip would continue on in some form— but my drive was done, and the realization moved through me like a melancholy wave.

Back then, I felt the heavy everywhere, and it was with me in the pub that night. The girl on the barstool to my right had a journal and a rocks glass Sorvino helped her keep full. Her name was Amelia Jean, and over the course of my hours there, she offered up glimpses into her world, one that felt strangely familiar. At first, I wondered if it was myself I saw in Amelia, the way she moved between her notebook and her glass. There was a loneliness I recognized in her, but when she tilted a scribbled note in my direction that read simply, "be a good little sol-dier," I realized it was Kelly she reminded me of—a woman privately fighting someone else's war. Of course, I couldn't know if this was true for Amelia, but it's easy when you travel to make people what you need them to be. So many nights I had been willing to investigate the heart-ache of strangers, to stand in the cold with fans who had been sick like me and offer them my kindness, but somehow, I couldn't do the same for Kelly. But she was off to Paris and I was about to fly south, and everything unsettled would have to wait.

I was tired, but the drive had been good for me. It's not that my leaving home was noble, but it reminded me I could stand without the structures I had come to rely on. And while my peace would be temporary, I knew there was peace to be had. I stayed at the pub until closing, scrawling notes in a moleskin to make sense of the ride, and then retired to a little hotel on East Franklin Street, where I slept off the drink and woke up in the morning inspired.

You could feel the ghosts in the rooms at the Linden Row Inn, and I felt at home in the company of ghosts. The hotel had been restored years prior, but try as you might, you can't take the creaking from the floorboards of an ancient thing. Like the crater blasted in terra firma, the inn was a relic preserved for people like me: a reminder that some history is, at best, worth preserving and, at worst, impossible to deny. I spent another full day there, circling my Craigslist keyboard and compiling my road trip into a song. I wrote that song for Kelly, but I called it "Amelia Jean." Then, with the snow falling, I loaded my car onto a trailer bound for home. I had considered returning to drive it back myself, but my marriage wouldn't survive another change of plans. I spent one more night at the pub with Sorvino and with the spirits at the Linden Row Inn. Then I boarded a plane in the morning bound for Costa Rica.

Day 10—Too Much Sun and a Drug Deal in the Jungle

I met Manhead in the hurly-burly of the Liberia airport closing down for the night, and after renting a car, we drove to the coast on dirt roads under canopies of blacked-out stars. By the time we made it through the jungle, we were whiplashed and buzzed on Imperials. Back then, Nosara was a sleepy expat town, known for the surfable waves that broke consistently at its sandy doorstep, but the impulse I had followed there didn't account for the restlessness I would feel upon landing. Richmond was a well-written ending; the time there had pointed me toward my record and home, and while I was grateful for the sun and the company of a friend, I grew more anxious with every perfect passing day. There were families walking dogs on the beaches while the rest of the world was at work. We ate gallo pinto every morning before surfing or lying by the pool, and though it was paradise, something about it felt like hell to me.

I didn't see it coming, I never did, but the cycle was always the same. The feeling that I'm not where I'm supposed to be, followed by the imposter sensation and the fear: fear of the cancer coming back, fear of the tasks before me, fear of dying or of living having lost my edge, fear I've chosen all the wrong roads, with no hope of return. By the fourth night in Costa Rica, I was keeling, lost in my headphones and second-guessing every sound I had made and word I had written. Had the hope I had carried with me from California to Virginia dried up in those final days of sun? I needed to pull myself together. Pot had been my crutch for years, but I was crutchless, so Manhead and I split a six-pack and the hit of ecstasy he accidentally traveled with and then we drove into town looking for trouble.

We found the right people with the wrong drugs, and they led us to a compound behind a guarded gate where I bought cocaine off a man with a machete. We had been drinking with two college kids back at the hotel and had brought them along for the ride. They were a Canadian couple in their early twenties, and they reminded me of how Kelly and I had once been, before the breakup and the cancer and our days of clouds and resistance. For a moment, things were dire—a group was gathering around our car, and it seemed we had stumbled into a trap. The girl in the backseat was bawling and ratcheting up the tension, she swore she had seen a gun, but I was too fixated on the machete, the drug deal, and the restless group surrounding us to follow her down that rabbit hole. Her boyfriend did what he could to keep her panic contained inside the rented SUV, but it wouldn't be long before her cries found their way from the car to the men outside. Sensing this, Manhead was preparing to back through the gate, but he managed to stay calm long enough for me to finish the deal, and the crowd eventually dispersed, and we departed. In the end, we made it out with our lives and some decent drugs, but the hair-raising transaction woke the death wish in me. The rest of my trip was a blur of drunk jungle drives, pulling doses to my nose from the back of my hand—just because I could. This was my life on the merry-go-round—I would hang on until it stopped spinning, for the sake of my art and my marriage, but I lost a few years along the way.

On the twenty-second of January, after five days on the beach, Manhead and I drove the dirt roads and rough highways in reverse, and boarded flights to separate coasts. Whether he got what he needed from his trip I couldn't say. In my case, it seems the road was a mirror to life as I was finding it. Some days I understood my place in the order of things; other days, I got stoned and climbed into a hole in the ground. On the worst days, I gave in, looking for a rush to keep me level, only to find myself confronting a void no rush could fill. We are who we are. Wonderful creatures of darkness and light. I got lost in the dark a lot those days, but I did what I could to write it down and sing it when I found the strength to. And in October of 2008, I released my bizarre little album about surviving in a world I hadn't yet made sense of. I called it *The Glass Passenger*.

Chapter 33

Floating with the Dead

I leaned on you like I leaned on everyone, with all my weight, and though you took it without asking questions, some days you wound up injured, your frailty condemned by those who refused to understand you. But I wouldn't listen to them. Days that would have otherwise consumed me I knew myself only in the hours we took flight, so I fought to keep you well when others lost faith. Maybe a family or some choir teacher could have given you a better life, but it seemed to me we were born to travel this world together. We understood each other's weaknesses, but instead of passing judgment, we shored them up with accommodating strength, aware we were better together than apart. Understanding all this, of course, would take time, but as I slowly emerged from the wreckage that you must have thought your home, my affection for you only grew deeper.

♫

Consciousness. I woke up slowly...not the good kind—those teenage Saturday mornings with the sun climbing as your sheets steal you from the day. This was hangover slow with places to be, and it mustered the remains of my Catholic guilt.

It was September of '09 when I first rented the guesthouse in the backyard of a Laguna Beach potter. I had been on the road for the better part of eighteen months supporting *The Glass Passenger*, and like the creation of the album itself, the touring had led me down rabbit holes into wasted dead ends. I spent my days in interviews with journalists, reliving the cancer my album so clearly reflected, and I spent my nights onstage and in the bars attempting to prove I was more alive than I had been before I fell ill. But the truth is I wasn't, and I was growing more worried every day that I was choosing to bury myself in a similar darkness to the one my father had chosen when I was young. I knew something needed to change—and with the tour ending in the UK and time off on the horizon, returning to Los Angeles felt like a death sentence.

When I boarded the plane home from London, I was still drunk from the night before, and I spent my time in the sky curled up and sick. Kelly retrieved me from baggage claim, and I fought the shakes in her passenger seat as we made the drive south. Laguna Beach is a hippie holdout from the '60s, and though no hippies can afford to live there any longer, it flies a liberal flag in a county still drunk on Ronald Reagan. It wasn't far from the towns where Kelly and I grew up, and I had rented us a house there, attempting to break the pattern of wild tours capped off by wild homecomings. We carved through the canyon with its steep hay-colored hills, then joined the traffic on Main Street, where the first sight of white water and sand drew breath into my body and its all-too-familiar ache: alcohol and sleeplessness, the spackle of oblivion. I was tired of the feeling.

We worked our way north on Coast Highway, parked, and then ascended the stairs to a brick and shiplap cottage to find its owner, Paulette, waiting in the courtyard. It was as if I had known her all my life. Her skin was radiant, well-worn, and her white-blonde hair traveled down her slender back like water falling. We toured the garden and the guesthouse, which would become our unexpected second home, the place we would return to as we plotted our escape from Los Angeles. And though she never said a word about the looks of me, Paulette seemed tuned to the frequency of my repair, insisting that I change into a swimsuit and then walking Kelly and me down to the beach.

I wasn't sure about getting in the water at first. It was late afternoon, and the chill was already in the air. To the uninitiated, Southern California is a year-round paradise of warm water and blistering sun, but when its subtle seasons turned, I felt them in my bones as deeply as the seasons of my youth. I looked out at the ocean, which was dressed in sequins by the nearly autumn sun, and to the sound of Kelly and Paulette, mystics trading histories, I pressed my feet into the sand, let my legs carry me to the shoreline, then dove beneath the crashing waves.

I had grown accustomed to the slideshow in my mind, a glitchy film of incoherent memories. It was worse when I woke up poisoned, as I did that day, but lying back into the hands of the Pacific, eyes fixed on the clouds above, the projectionist took pity on me, offering up an image I could use. I disappeared into the scene, and as I did, I felt my worry leaving. Not far from me but a world away, a man, barely older than I was, lay floating on the surface of green water, my uncle Stuart. I could see him; I could feel his presence there. Before the cancer had forced him into a hospital bed, this was his ocean, and these were his waves, and with my eyes closed I could feel him floating next to me. I never knew my uncle Stuart as a man, but my music was his music and his disease had become mine. Only I had been the one to survive. I wondered to myself, what was this life of mine without floating? What were these late-night simulations of near death that often chased me into the morning? I closed my eyes once more, surrendered to the water, and it rocked me like a child in its arms. The ocean is unpredictable, but if you study how it moves—keeping track of the tides and their affair with the moon almighty—you, too, can float eyes closed out where the waves break. Stuart was there, then he was gone, but the color had returned to my skin, and my body ceased its shaking.

It's not that everything changed at once, but just as the beach had become my home after my family's forced migration, it called me once again, offering redemption where there had been despair. From that day until the following new year, Kelly and I would continue to return to Paulette, her cottage, and the beach. There I began writing the music that became Jack's Mannequin's third and final album, a study in conflict and love.

Chapter 34

TARANTULA MATING SEASON

My remaining days in the band were focused less on the furthering of my career and more on mitigating the harm I'd done pursuing it. The paranoid warfare of my cancer recovery had found its first casualties in my managers, Arvis and Carl. The journey from client to patient had left me hobbling on my return, and though they had done most everything right, I felt I had to move on if I was going to keep moving. I needed space from the person I had been in those blind, fighting days, but my bandmates would see my decision differently. I had fired friends and replaced them with outsiders who couldn't make sense of the piece-meal agreements by which the four of us were governed. The band and I had had our differences in the past, but this was a new kind of suspicion, and it put pressure on our relationships until the end.

Jon was the next to leave. At the time, I blamed him for changing, for giving up on us and refusing to fall in line. He had been missing flights and coming to practice angry, and, in a time when I could have extended him some empathy, tried to understand where he was coming from, I was simply too exhausted to deal. The truth is, I was the one who was changing. I had led us through the fields of chaos only to turn my back and insist on order. I felt like a heretic, attempting to correct the trajectory of the unruly machine I had built and asked everyone to board—but something had to give. The business was unsustainable. A couple of months off the road was enough to bleed my bank account dry, and at a time when I needed the grounding of home, I couldn't shake the feeling of being trapped inside my own creation. And like the mapless road I traveled to get there, there would be no clear way out.

Despite the shifting dynamics, Raw, JayMac, and I held it together, and in the fall of 2010 we began work on our third and final album. We lived two seasons in the desert in Joshua Tree, learning the new songs, drinking absinthe, and waiting for the tarantulas to come out at night. The label rented us a modern house that sat alone in the Martian terrain at the bottom of a rocky hill. We kept our gear set up in the living room, playing from morning until night, and hiking into the red desert at the property's edge when the music stopped making sense. The songs I was writing then were about tension, the desire to break free, and about my turbulent first years of marriage—those nights with catastrophic endings and mornings when Kelly and I woke up just to watch the sun rise. We weren't out of the woods yet, but there was enough distance to appreciate how hard she and I had fought to stay together. That fight and the love it required became the songs that JayMac, Raw, and I were learning in those desert sessions.

When the band and I first began work on the record, Jessie, Kelly, and Jen would visit us in Joshua Tree on the weekends, but you could sense the ground beneath the six of us was shifting. We were still a family, but we were learning to keep our armor close, and in that sense, we became the kind of family I understood. My cancer was a trauma we all shared; it had been central to our collective story from the start. But the six of us were moving past those strange days, taking stock of their impact, and as we did, each of us claimed a little distance for ourselves.

The truth is, the business between the band and I had grown complicated, the way most relationships do over time. The perfect storm of new management, a departing member, and an album to record made it challenging for the three of us to find common ground. We made it work in the end, but our wives took sides along the way, and by the time they reached our corners, they had drifted too far from one another for things to ever be the same again. Their sisterhood, our family dinners, and nights in the neighborhood bars were becoming the exception rather than the rule. Painful as it was to watch Kelly's support system collapse, we had begun leaning on each other again, and together we decided to seek a future less affected by the ebb and flow of my business and the friendships caught up in it. And while there were so many moments when I could have done better by her and by the band, those days and the realizations born of them were the beginning of a healing chapter, one that would find Kelly and me back on stable ground.

With autumn coming to an end, the band and I moved out of the desert and into a warehouse studio north of Los Angeles, where we made our final record together. An album I called *People and Things*. When I hear those songs now, I see the house in Joshua Tree and the three of us recording in a room with tapestry walls. I see passport stamps and stage lights, I hear airplanes taking off and fights about money, I see Jen and Kelly on a dance floor in Japan, and Jessie buying rounds in the Silverlake bars knowing we've all had too much to drink. And like a collective fingerprint, the lives we'd lived as bandmates and friends were pressed down on the tape of each studio take as we created one last collection of songs. In the end, we made an album about marriage and relationships, about how much harder it is to hold on to love than you think it will be. Raw and JayMac had been witnesses at my wedding, and I'd been a witness at theirs. And regardless of our differences along the way, a record about family—and fighting for love—seemed a fitting piece of music for the three of us to call our last.

In the final months of 2010, Kelly and I sold our house in Los Angeles, and on New Year's Eve, after weeks of searching for a new place to live, we drove south to see a home in the heart of the town we fled years before. We had done our time in the hill house with the green roof and the treehouse with the earthbound stars, and we had lived our life in the city. But with our days there mired in struggle and so many of our friendships strained, we had run out of reasons to stay. Kelly and I had moved to Los Angeles, attempting to put space between us, the break-up, and the hospital—memories we had hoped to leave behind. What we found in the end was that trying to escape a memory is like feeding oxygen to a fire. Maybe leaving Los Angeles was just another version of running away, but if there were hard times ahead, we wanted to face them at home.

We exited the freeway and drove through the streets of the town where we had dated, broken up, gotten sick, and gotten better, and when we pulled into the driveway of a Spanish bungalow for sale, we knew—before we stepped out of the car—that we had found our own little place by the water. We made an offer on the spot, the owners accepted, and then we drove to the harbor to ring in the new year with old friends.

Trejo was managing the bar that night, having returned from his time in Las Vegas. I liked watching him work—he was rough on the high school kids, the stoned busboys and the oblivious hostesses who took personal calls on company time. We were pushing thirty, I had spent most of my adult life entertaining teenagers—and they still scared me to death. Not Trejo. He walked the room like a politician, issuing orders, shaking hands with the regulars, and taking shots behind the bar when no one was looking.

The place was a legendary harbor dive, but despite its prime water-front real estate, Harpoon Henry's served stiff drinks to a humble crowd. Our friend's dad had been the owner for decades, and little had changed there in all those years. The ceilings were shiplap, the carpets green, and the walls were home to fishing spears and paintings of sail-ors and sailboats tilting at the wind. Ten years prior, in that very same bar, I asked Kelly to be my girlfriend. We made the most important decision of our lives in the dark that night while a lounge singer did his best Elvis. His name was Phil Shane: he had a black pompadour and hauled a rack of sequin jackets with him everywhere he went. And as fate would have it, he would be taking the same stage in the dining room shortly.

One by one, our crew filtered in through the bar's swinging side door, and Daniels and Brent were among them. There is a rare comfort in the company of old friends. To have been loved in braces and baby fat, to walk the aisle at graduation and again at one another's weddings, is a kind of brotherhood I never dreamed of as a kid. But there we were, friends with history and nothing to hide. Just beyond the walls of the bar was the harbor where we used to smoke bad cigars after Saturday night joyrides. Those teenage nights we traded stories over the soundtrack of boats creaking in their dock slips and ropes battering masts in the wind. I can't hear those sounds now without thinking of freshman year, of my family's little blue townhouse on the bluff or my room with the Japanese screens. I had been traveling all my life, but I understood what it meant to be home. And in that bar full of boat people, drunk Republicans, and hipsters at home with their irony, we waited for midnight and the new year. Then Kelly and I raised our glasses to the friends who knew us best, to the days we were too lost to be known, and to the hope that those days were behind us.

The night ended in the guesthouse at Paulette's, where we had been crashing for the holidays. Kelly helped me out of my clothes and into bed. I wasn't drunk enough to need it, but she was kind enough to oblige. She lifted the sweater from my outstretched arms with a caution no longer required. The muscle memory of the helper and the helped is not so easily undone. All the baths she had drawn and the skin she had bandaged for me, all those days as my pillar and my shield. We had traveled through the worst of it. The fear and destruction, the misplaced blame and hidden truths, all the miracles of science and faith.

Sometimes the whole of those blistering years hit us both at once. All it took was a picture or a song, and we were surrounded by the vastness of the life we had shared. And with the cold climbing through the cracks in the cottage windows, we were grateful for the promise of better days. We fell back on the bed, wrapped ourselves in blankets, and fell asleep to the sound of our own laughter.

Chapter 35

I Was the Diver, It Was Our World

Kelly took possession of our bungalow on Valentine's Day 2011 while I was in Australia on tour. Paulette met her there, and together they decorated each room with subtle nods to the cottage, which had been central to our hope, renewed. During our time in her guesthouse, we had grown fond of Paulette and came to think of her as our fairy godmother. The calm we enjoyed as her tenants had fueled our desire to move back home. This new house was everything we had never imagined for ourselves—a 1927 lath and plaster relic with a clay tile roof, parked in the shade of an ancient Christmas tree. And while our early months there would be a reprieve from the patterns in which we had been locked, old troubles would flower inside those brawny walls, and it would be our work to finally cut them down.

Kelly and I were back in the orbit of the friends and family who knew us best. The depth of those connections and their ties to our personal history reflected back the parts of us that had hardened in our time away. It cannot be understated just how blindly we navigated my cancer and how profoundly it altered our lives. For Kelly's part, she had walked every mile of that road with me, felt every second of every bad day, shed every tear, and celebrated every clean bill of health and anniversary that passed in remission, but those who care for the compromised are too often overlooked. Few people bothered to investigate how Kelly was holding up in the midst of our trials, least of all me, her husband. And when the recovery proved to be a sickness of its own, one that drove us into hiding—so ashamed we couldn't make our way through gracefully—it also injured the hope and faith that had made the cancer survivable. I had stopped believing in myself and stayed high to take the edge off the grieving. Kelly protected me—the same way my mother protected my father—paying lip service to how lucky we were, spinning optimistic half-truths at cocktail parties or backstage after shows. I knew what she was doing, covering for me, afraid the truth might force her hand if she heard it spoken aloud. But that's what we did: we put on a good face and kept moving, the happy couple who had made it through hell with so few scars. But the scars were there, and they were many, we knew it; we just hadn't figured out what to do with them yet.

It's difficult to write these words knowing how so many don't survive their cancer. As a public figure thrust into the role of advocacy, I became close with a number of patients, and too many times I cried behind sunglasses at funerals where young people were laid to rest. Unable to find my footing in the world, the guilt I felt for surviving was profound, and it lived within me like an organ or an aching tooth. I carried with me a constant sense of shame. I was living recklessly on my second chance, stoned from morning to night, drinking daily, and no stranger to a short list of harder drugs. And while our move down the coast and out of Los Angeles tempered some of my worst inclinations, the root cause still begged to be treated or pacified. Those early months in our new home were anything but easy, but in the end, I would be grateful for our little house by the water because, for the first time, there was no place to run. No studio nearby, no industry events, or house parties. Just Kelly and me, and a town full of people we loved and leaned on as we surfaced from the years we spent submerged.

By the middle of that first summer, our fighting had gotten worse. The black dog of depression was with me always, corrupting my belief in time and healing. I could still get out of bed, but so many days I lay there wondering what for. I saw a future with my band dismantled and spent my days, uninspired, staring at the keys of a piano that wouldn't play for me.

At the same time, Kelly was finding her voice. She had always been strong, but she had put her faith in me, that I would return to her the way I had once been, and it kept her from putting me on trial. But with her twenties in the rearview, she had a right to know if I was ever going to step up and be the husband she deserved. I wasn't ready to answer questions about my mental health, my anger, or my choice to meet the day impaired, but she was done sharing the house with a ghost. The harder she pushed back on me, the more explosive our exchanges became.

There were tire marks in the driveway, empty threats of divorce, and then one sweltering night in September, I climbed up on my soapbox with some bullshit defense to her well-earned concerns. She burned that soapbox down. She was done. It had been six years since the hospital, and good days be damned, I had never returned to her, never fully recovered. I was a cynic, a stoner, and cruel in confrontation. I stayed out late and didn't call and left her to worry about where I was and whom I'd fallen in with so many nights as I moved through the world. She knew where I came from and feared me steering toward addiction and felt like a fool for having accepted my excuses for years. I had robbed her of her youth and then asked for loyalty in return. She had loved me through it all, but she couldn't love me any longer, not like that. And that night in September, she finally gave me an ultimatum: either I find my way back to the land of the living or she was moving on without me.

I was in shock, suspended between the ceiling and the floor, the vintage fixtures and bullnose archways—a room in a house I thought would do the fixing for me. Everything was silent but the fan overhead. We were standing at the intersection. How many summers had we shared since our bonfire beginnings, when we were kids, and everything was possible? The first tour buses and punk rock shows, our buzz-cut breakup and hospital reconciliation, the treehouse packed with eccentrics and friends, and all the warmest months of the year since. We wouldn't survive another September split. Kelly knew it and so did I.

In the kitchen, the clock hands reached for midnight, but all I could think about were her eyes. In our years of pining letters, those eyes had been forests and jade pools, clover meadows, and hole-punched myrtle coins, but as I traced the floor in shame to then find those eyes looking through me, all I could see was the fire and the white and the truth I'd been denying for years. She had given everything to me, and I had been nothing but careless with the both of us. Exhausted, she retired to the bedroom, her voice, an engine, flooded, while I carved through the trapped heat in the hall, pacing, until my batteries ran out.

For years, I had wrested control, let the wild wind carry me, but I had lost my bearings in the sky. I let my cancer own me in the aftermath, as if it never left my body. All the gifts I had been given that had saved me from my sick days and my father's addiction—my optimism and ambition, my dreaming and faith in a song—I had relegated them all to a shadow, for fear they could be taken without warning. I see it now, I surrendered in advance, straddling the line between trying and trying not to get my hopes up. Whether it was a record or a tour or the marriage I now stood to lose, I was never fully present, too afraid to go all in. I had seen where it could lead—faith in loved ones who let you down, the sacrifice of everything only to wind up a poisoned patient with your dreams on hold. So I hedged my bets. I did the work, but I set traps everywhere I went: for Kelly, for the band, for myself, and for the people who believed in me. I didn't know what I was doing, but I knew it was wrong; that night in the living room, with the hot air turning and the clock hands ticking away, I took it all on for the first time because I had to. Because Kelly was everything to me, and I didn't want to go through life without her. She had thrown me a parachute, had given me a place to land, and in refusing to lose her, I would be forced to recover myself. As I stood gutted in that September heat, I had a choice to make.

While she slept, I searched the web for hope and answers, and then I sent out my SOS; by morning, I was face-to-face with the doctor who would guide me through a journey of grief and forgiveness. One I had waited far too long to take. My eyes were bloodshot from a night without sleep, but I knew what I was there to do, and I was ready. It was time to let go, to see what life is like when the secrets breathe.

"So…"

The therapist swallowed as if standing at the diving board's edge.

"What brings you here?"

But I was the diver, and what came next was the rest of my life.

Chapter 36

People
and
Things

This was the year I took it easy on you. Was I playing it safe, not tram-pling your keys underfoot, or was the abandonment of my persona, "the breaker of things," one final act of rebellion?

♬

In October 2011, *People and Things* was released, and the band and I took to the road with a new bass player. We called him Mikey the Kid. He was 120 pounds of effortless thrift store cool and quick with his fists when provoked. I loved having him around. Just like it had been when Raw joined Something Corporate, Mikey helped us put our differences aside for a time. We played nearly two hundred concerts in support of the new album, and though he never let it show onstage, Raw was on his way out. I recognized the look in his eyes. I had worn him down the way I had worn down others, and despite traveling in close quarters, the nearer we got to the end, the less I saw of him. The tour bus would park at the venue in the morning, and he would rush off to the hotel or a coffee shop. The show would end, and we'd leave for the bar and he would find another place to drink. In a way it was worse than fighting...though we did a bit of that, too.

When the tour ended, we met in a café and said the things we should have said long before. Despite his signature calm, when it came to business, Raw's voice always shook—his cadence was contagious, and we exchanged our trembling language to the finish. He had been ready to leave the band for some time, and his desire to break free had turned the road into a prison for him. I don't remember the particulars: if there were demands I wouldn't meet or if we both arrived knowing we were done. What I do remember is the café itself. It was packed, the kind of place where hard conversations hide easily. The woodwork was a shade darker than walnut, and our table was fixed to the boundary of a busy thoroughfare where servers with trays full of food muscled past patrons on their way to the restrooms and the exits. Raw had his back to the front door, and the sun flooding in obscured his place in our parting. From what I recall, neither of us was angry, just aware that we had traveled together as far as we could. The exchange was an autopsy, a funeral, and the gift of being born again. And when it ended, we stepped into the world untethered. Jack's Mannequin had been mine in the beginning, but it had become ours. And without Raw it belonged to the past. From the apartment in Beverly Hills with the dead-strain acid in the fridge to the band house on Sunset Boulevard and nights at the Thirsty Crow. From Beethoven on ecstasy to heavy metal in the bus's front lounge. From bruised arms and black eyes to run-ins with police—our journey together had been unquestionably epic.

I left the café first, into the daylight of a decades-old picture, lobotomized...unfeeling. There is an emptiness in a mutual parting. When two sides surrender, all that's left are the hollow insides of a trophy neither will carry. Our collaboration had been the most enduring of my career. We could not have been more different or more complementary—but each of us had things to prove, and our reliance on each other called into question whether we could make it on our own. We could and we did. I knew I would miss him. I wasn't sure if he would feel the same, but ultimately, we remained friends, and in the end, I would be as grateful for that as any song we made or crowd we left wanting more.

Chapter 37

THE
VAMPIRE
ON
MELROSE

Summer 2012: I'm sitting on a white couch in a white room. The television is white, the counters, the floors and the ceiling...white. The piano, the dog, and three concrete pots holding miniature palm trees that will never reach maturity...all white. After the last tour with Jack's Mannequin, I left my unanswered questions to hang in the air. What's next and where will the money come from? In the absence of answers, I waited. I hadn't been so still in years, and when I started feeling guilty, I had my publisher and ex-party accomplice, Ron, throw me into the fire of the Los Angeles songwriting scene. "Replace your fear with faith." I repeat it like a mantra in the whitewashed room. The phrase—a gift from my therapist, the only doctor I see now—has carried me through a year of endings and unknowns. Without those words, this room does not exist.

The session was scheduled for noon, then got bumped to three o'clock. I came back at three to find it pushed to four. It's five now, and I'm feeling like a guest in a hotel lobby waiting for a room. I don't mind. The house is a piece of performance art, and fighting my nerves to avoid puking on the colorless furniture seems like a worthy contribution to the scene.

The owner of this place has not one but three assistants, all attractive young women. Their charm is undeniable, three sterling personalities free of the self-consciousness that plagues their generation. Each has her own unique style not yet corrupted by the beige assimilation that, for most of us, comes with age. One is tall with bleached hair, piercings, and punk vestiges, but she wears them inoffensively, borrowed in the name of fashion. The other two are smaller, wearing loose-fitting tank tops and poorly concealed bras, and they check in on me throughout the long wait. We speak occasionally while they proceed through a lengthy list of tasks, making calls, trading gossip, and at one point, nearly setting fire to the kitchen.

I've parted ways with my band, my managers, and my record company, and it's been months without a ringing phone. My therapy year has been a gauntlet: the confrontation of a life and the patterns born of trauma. It's been good for Kelly and me, but it's been hard, too, making peace with squandered time. Still, I try to focus on the day, and as I feel myself returning, the cancer and what came after have taken on the air of an impossible dream. I know they are not, I confront the reality daily, but I do so with gratitude, knowing Kelly and I have made it through to the other side. I am nowhere near fixed and have stopped believing such a destination exists. Not for me anyway. So I do the work. I apologize when I can, I dispense forgiveness if I'm able, and, slowly, I clear the forest brush hoping for a quiet fire season and new growth in the spring. When I told my publisher that I was ready to work again, this house full of assistants with no producer in sight was not exactly what I had imagined, which, I suppose, makes it a perfect place to start. Good art is rarely born of comfort, which bodes well for me, because these days I am far from comfortable.

When the king finally emerges, he is gaunt, ghost white (shocking, I know), and styled from foot to crown in expensive sneakers and

carefully destroyed hair. There is a vampire quality to this man, supported further by his rising with the moon. His name is Fernando, and
he is at once nothing and everything I expected. He checks in with his
army of assistants, drinks coffee, and is now gathering steam. And while
I have no reason to trust him, I immediately do.

We walk from the house to the studio, past the palm trees and the
men who care for them. The assistants talk over one another in the distance, but I can't make out what they're saying. I'm wrestling with the
voices telling me to run, to give up before I write a single note or word,
but I find the mute button, reminding myself how bad things got when
I let those voices steer. We proceed through the studio door, passing a
small lounge, bathed in the beryl blue light of an aquarium, and the
sight of water reminds me to breathe.

Finally, in a room like a spaceship, we exchange histories. Fernando's
an EDM kid with ties to Giorgio Moroder, the godfather of the electronic movie score, and he's recently landed massive hits with Lady
Gaga. My résumé is an exercise in contrast, but launching two successful acts and staying relevant for more than a decade is not without its
merits, and Fernando makes me feel worthy of his time.

Over the next several months, we will work together regularly—he
will be both my champion and tough-talking coach, insisting I write
words worthy of the stars he hopes will sing them. A couple of our
songs will be put on hold by big names, but, in the end, not one will
be recorded. It doesn't matter though—the long nights and hours commuting will be worth it. From Fernando, I will learn how to write with
my back against the wall, and when applied to my own music, it will
lead to the success I had only dreamed of as a boy.

Chapter 38

New Friends
and a
Night in Las Vegas

I never realized how many roads there were to a song until I finally stepped off the one I had been traveling all those years.

We were drifting apart. Like the pianos I played before you, all the miles forged, and trials witnessed, would live forever in your wooden hull like the rings of an aging tree. But the road you were born on would have to wait, and the family you were born into needed rest and time to heal. I had no space for you at home any longer; I had culled my appetite for hideouts and houses with more rooms than I could use, so you rested in the same dark valley closet where, years before, I'd retired your predecessor. You wouldn't be there for long, but our writing days were done, and like so many friends from my years of troubled mending, we would meet again and recalibrate our bond.

♫

Mark Williams was a twenty-year-old prodigy from Pittsburgh. We met in a studio in the basement of a Hollywood high-rise, where he sat dwarfed by the gear in his command. He was pale, thin, and looked like he had dressed himself in clothes pulled from a pile on the floor of a bedroom with a blow-up mattress. (Oh, to be twenty again.) Combined with his head of errant dark curls, the effect rendered him a misfit professor, which, in the end, was a fitting portrayal. I had been working late with Fernando the previous evening, had gone out for drinks with friends and was moving slowly that day. By the time we started making noise, I had only recovered by a small percentage, but Mark worked while I pulled myself together, saving my strength as I sat cheering him on from a couch in the corner. Little by little, his construction drew me upright, until finally I made my way into the vocal booth with the muse closing in.

I had never written music that way, staring through the control room glass at a stranger, but over the next few hours, Mark and I moved through complementary orbits, building a song like kids build castles in sand: wrapped up in the simple joy of assembly. What met me in the frenzy of creation was a history I had only recently found the strength to confront: a portrait of my sister and I moving through time, our adolescence marred by addiction, and our twenties a maze of leukemia and mental illness. On your best days as a writer, you locate within yourself windows of hidden truth, and on that afternoon a window opened, reminding me of what Kate and I had survived. My road back had been circuitous, but I had made it. Kate had been healthy for years and had channeled her intellect and discipline into a successful career and a life of purpose. And in a moment both prophetic and profound, the musical arrangement fell to pieces, and forgiveness claimed me in the amber light. The piano landed, a ripple in a once-still pond, and I saw my parents there, not for their flaws, but for the gift they gave my brothers, my sisters, and me. Our many houses had been visited by tragedy, but even at their most compromised, my parents never gave up, and my siblings and I marched through time to an unfaltering drumbeat of love. Their love. The image spun itself into words, and I sang them as if

I were alone, but I was not. On the other side of the glass sat a kid with a gift I would come to revere, and together we would make a suite of songs about overcoming, reconciliation, and the unbreakable bonds of family.

A few days later, Kelly and I traveled to Las Vegas to watch Fernando DJ. I had never been a club kid, but my "days of new" had lifted me from the heavy of years passed, so I said yes, and we hopped on a plane to spend a night in the entourage. Fernando took dinner with a laptop and his headphones on, preparing for the show, while Kelly and I made small talk with his assistants. And when the time came, security walked us through the casino to a red rope island in the shadow of Fernando's waiting dais. What was this world I had stumbled into? Booths and bottle service, low lights and lasers cutting through dense sheets of fog. I would have felt ridiculous if I weren't having so much fun. And when the man of the hour took control of the room, there was nothing left to do but surrender.

All at once, my blood was flooded, bounding toward the intersection of music and the invention of memory. Kelly wore the color of the club lights on her skin, and I couldn't get close enough to her if I tried. She had saved me, but more than that, she insisted I become what she deserved—and I felt worthy with my arms around her. *What we had lived through mattered.* From the breakup to the hospital to those houses on hills and everything that came before and after. So many times we could have given up, walked away for good, but we fought through it for nights like this, and for the good life we were finally living. All the messiness and devotion had led us to that undulating room, and we moved through it, half collapsed on each other, half floating, as the DJ, my brief mentor and friend, drilled deeper into the nostalgic core. And when the island couldn't hold us any longer, we swam the sea of dance floor bodies, hypnotized by the songs, a symphony of deft curation.

I don't remember how we exited the club. One moment Kelly and I were dancing, and the next we were back in our hotel room whispering on a tangle of bed sheets. The story of most American cities and towns began with settlers in search of a better life pursuing some unmet need. In the late nineteenth century, Las Vegas had water in a desert where there was little, and during the Depression, it had jobs when there were few—and as Kelly and I looked out on its plastic skyline, the neon paint splashed across the walls of our room, I thought of the city and how I had used it to mark time. Vegas had been a symbol of freedom first navigated on a fake ID. A land of birthdays and bachelor parties, it was the brief home of my closest friend and a refuge in times of unthinkable pressure. But as my eyes shifted from the unholy circus outside, back to Kelly and our knotted limbs, I had a feeling that city and that night were about to mean more. I moved naked through the dark to find my phone, and then, washed in colors from the strip below, we listened to a song. The one I had written in the high-rise with Mark. Through the buzz I heard the future of my music, but it was *our* future I was listening for. The crude work tape climbed from the cell phone speaker while I scribbled notes on hotel stationery, so afraid I'd lose the scene in my once-radiated brain. I tracked Kelly's green eyes as we rounded the second chorus where the arrangement came undone. Then rising through the quiet came the words...

> Now we live our own lives
> But in the night when my spirit's drifting
> And I come up from the deep end dive
> I see the eyes of my unborn children
> And I'm filled with the love I will give them
> Cause it's the love I was given

Life is just a series of moments; the most consequential are often camouflaged in the menagerie. But some moments, however rare, dispense of protocol, stalling the clock hands just long enough to catalog the angles of a room, the language as it crashes and climbs. How lucky

I was to be so alive, to have lived so hard, to love so much and have been so loved. Kelly and I froze time that night, pulled the paper from the walls and reconstructed that hotel room in our memories. All the furniture and mass-produced artwork, the carpet, the mirrors, and the messed-up sheets. Somehow, we knew we would want to return, not to that place at some later date and time but to that exact moment. The one where, briefly, we saw into the future. We were family and our family would soon grow.

Chapter 39

WRECKING BALL, REST IN PEACE

I played my final show as Jack's Mannequin on November 12, 2012, at the El Rey Theatre in Los Angeles. I had grown up seeing shows there, spent countless teenage nights pressed against its barricade with my friends in the scrum, worshipping like zealots on a Sunday. It was the right place to say goodbye: a farewell to the faithful in a room where I learned to pray.

By then, Jack's Mannequin belonged to the fans. It was their cities and venues, their bars and hotels I haunted for years, not knowing who I was at home. All that was over, but I felt a debt to them, for believing in me when privately I struggled to believe in myself. Sometimes I wonder what would have happened if I allowed for more time between the cancer and my return. If I had removed all the hooks and splinters first, would I have patched up my mind as quickly as the doctors patched up my body? Or did I come back to life the way I did, rock-ribbed and rattling, because I couldn't stand to be away from those stages and that choir of a crowd? I'll never know, but I'm done wasting time on the question. Whatever it was, it had to be.

So we gathered at the El Rey and paid our respects to seven of the strangest years I'll ever know. By then, Bobby had moved to New York with Jen, and they flew in for the week. Jon was living in Richmond, and though it had been years since we parted ways, he returned to the club and to California to say his goodbyes as well. Jay and Mikey lived in Los Angeles, and we had plans to keep playing together when the time came, but that night at the El Rey, we were focused on the history we shared. I hired cameras and told our story, which to this day is still hard to believe: how a breakup and a batch of bedroom songs turned into a seven-year thesis on disease, survival, and the burden and beauty of love. How a side project grew into a body of work, a band of brothers and a family, and how even though it was ending, the music we made would be the proof of those wild years, survived. When we took the stage for the last time that night, we did so as friends, honoring the shapes and sounds we made together, then claiming ourselves when the curtain closed.

It was the kind of goodbye I couldn't write for Something Corporate. The weird soup of illness and ambition stole me from the task of our fond farewell. It still bothers me sometimes, but I suppose that's the price you pay for being young. So busy updating the dream I was constantly chasing, I failed to notice that the dream had actually come true. If I *had* noticed, I think I could have been the bandmate that Kevin, Brian, Josh, and Will deserved. I was born hungry and reaching, and though I turned my one true gift into a career, the loner in me too often lost sight of the human cost, the ecosystems that made it possible for me to thrive. I am far from perfect, but I see it clearly now—it is the people who have believed in me that are responsible for this thing I get to do. To make a living from my love of songs. And though I had made so many of the same mistakes on my second go-round, I knew better than to turn my back on Jack's Mannequin without saying goodbye.

Kelly and I met the band at St. Nick's after the show. Though it wasn't one of our usual spots, it reminded me of the dives we used to drink in, and stepping through the front door, I felt like we had walked into a theater at the end of a film. Inside, a long bar cut through the center of the room, which was dimly lit and lined with booths dressed in lipstick-red cushions. The place was packed. A gathering of souls from all corners of the world who felt the need, like me, to sing together one last time. Looking out over the crowded bar, I was reminded of my good fortune. So many kids dream of making music for a living, and there I was, ten years after signing my first record deal, having found success twice over. I was proud of what we built as Jack's Mannequin. Not just the band and I, but the fans who willed it into being. It was a collective, a family shrine to music and mending. I didn't notice the debris from which it climbed, nor was I worried about the shadows it might cast. It was a tower now, not the one I had set out to build, but it was substantial nevertheless, and more than I could have ever hoped for. We traded rounds and stories, knowing it might be the last time our crew would raise glasses in the clatter of a dive, and then just before last call, Kelly and I said our goodbyes and drove home. In the morning, a new life would be waiting.

Chapter 40

The
Wilderness
Years

Starting over at twenty is easy. At thirty it's a test of your mettle. I've thought about it a lot, the concept of reinvention. The term has been used both by me and by others to describe the way I've moved through my career and in some ways my life. My restlessness is a side effect of my upbringing, one of the greatest gifts my parents could have given me. And while I would argue that I'm just as afraid of change as anyone, I'm more afraid of standing still to find the world has moved on without me. As a kid, there was always hope waiting in the next city at the end of another long drive; difficult as it was sometimes to pack up and go, I found the unknown more intriguing than the known. I never make plans to start over, there are no calculations or incentives weighed. At worst, I've made a mess I'm trying to flee. At best, there's some new frontier or inspiration I can't help but chase down. But the truth is, most times, when I begin again, it's some combination of the two. I fear the plateau, I prefer the climb, but I'd rather descend, regroup, and find another mountain than keep watching the world from the same lookout, no matter how breathtaking the view.

In August 2013 I rented a hovel in Los Angeles's Topanga Canyon on a property littered with a half dozen shacks. Two of them you might have called houses, and another few were plywood boxes dressed up for weekend acid trips. But the one I liked best and chose to spend my time in was a cabin made of concrete and stone. It had an outhouse, a hot plate, and a lamp, and it sat on the back of the property where you wouldn't see a soul for days. I had climbed yet another hill, but this time not to hide. I was on a mission. After briefly managing myself and releasing songs independently to little fanfare, my hunger pains had returned. The temporary detour had been good for me, but I was ready to get back into the ring. I found managers I trusted—and their advice to me was to write, write, write. I knew I'd have one shot at establishing my name outside the shadow of my past success. So I spent the weeks behind a keyboard in solitude and my weekends at home with Kelly.

In the canyon I did nothing but make music and smoke cigarettes on the roof, occasionally wandering into town for food and a cell phone signal. I lived for the sunsets, but it took time to get used to the quiet that followed them. Is there anything louder than the absence of sound in the wild? When it got hot and the bed sheets stuck to me, I would throw the door open, and on the best nights, I would find the moon had laid its cool blue arms down on the canyon, the world asleep within its shivering monochrome.

Kelly was pregnant by then, but we had postponed our celebrations. She had miscarried earlier in the year, and when I traveled home from the cabin for her doctor's appointments, it took everything I had not to slide back into that ice water memory.

February 11, how I wish I could erase you. Cold jelly on the wand sent searching in the hallow of my darling's womb…the heartbeat we had learned to listen for had gone missing. The doctor bowed his head, leaving us alone to greet the paradox of emptiness and sinking. I remember staring out a window at a palm tree; how different it had looked when we arrived. And when the shock finally assimilated, I walked Kelly through the hall like a bodyguard, past the staff and half-full waiting room, down the elevator to the parking lot, where I fed her collapsing frame into the car. There would be one last sad procedure, another silent car ride through rust-colored hills, winter and still no sign of rain. We spent three weeks in bed, the sheets sometimes trembling atop our weeping bodies, but we would heal in time. We would buy a birdhouse and paint it gray and yellow, and then hang it in the garden so we would never forget. We never would.

As my time in Topanga Canyon came to an end, I was visited by a presence in my sleep. I had been falling, but not falling alone. I could sense it was the little girl who would one day find us, and unlike the soul we had grieved just months before, she would make it into her mother's arms and mine. The first song I wrote for her would be one of few to survive my days in the cabin of stone, but the self-reliance I learned there would prepare me for what came next. To be a writer is to write. What you keep or share is a conversation for another time—and in the days that followed, if I faltered or lost track of the muse, what I learned in that hovel in the canyon would sustain me.

I spent the rest of the year in a garage studio in Echo Park only miles from the house with the green roof that Kelly and I had sold in search of better days. The homes I've lived in live on in me, and that asylum on the hill, with its emerald slate walkway, was as close to Ardmore and Ohio as any I've known. So many nights before the baby came, I would find myself driving through Silverlake, past the bars where I used to drink, past the reservoir and Spaceland, up the stair streets to Silverwood Terrace and to the house where Kelly and I had ridden out our storm. I had been a ghost in that house—and my father and the cancer had been the ghost in me.

Months passed, and as my catalog of new songs grew, so did the child who would soon call *me* father. And on the days I couldn't help myself—parked outside that house with the green roof and wondering who I was within its walls—I hoped my daughter's ghosts would be her own and never mine.

Cecilia Kate was born the morning before Valentine's Day, 2014. She had her mother's eyes, only darker, and losing myself in them, I had finally found a reason for my hard-weather years: her, the luminous little being I took to calling C. To hold a creature of your blood is to travel in time, and on the day my parents first held Cecilia, I was stolen by our motion-sick history. All the moving trucks, fresh paint and new houses, the piano recitals and hospital rooms, the funerals and weddings, road trips and days on the edge. I felt their love and desperation, their pride and pipe dreams of time as an eraser, I saw the cigarette ash mountains and the orange marrow on ice, I took their gifts of muscle and bone. My parents' time had come and gone; they had done the best they could for me, and it was enough. It was my turn now, and for my daughter, I would do the same.

As Cecilia grew, I poured myself into the writing of a second song for her, one I had started with friends when I had only known her in my dreams. It took months to get the lyrics right, but we worked it like a canvas with patience and an eye on fate. In the end, the song was a map of my personal history, wrapped in a promise of protection, and after three bands and fifteen years on the road, it would become my first hit record.

Chapter 41

PEACE
in the Desert

I have to imagine you noticed the change in me. The color and the lift. Nearly a year had passed in your road-case waiting room, but the music and momentum that met us on the other side would prove that you were back in high demand. The scant budgets for your tuning and boggy months of summer weren't ideal for either of us, but it was better than leaving you at home. I made a prop of you once more, a second elevation from which I announced my return, and while we waited for the world to meet us there, my roly-poly little girl was never far away, for the lifting of spirits. I would prop her on your lid, feet barely scraping at the skyline of your black keys, and as they did, I made peace with the man you met in bruises. If those days were the cost of her company, I would live them ten times over again.

♬

Cecilia was five months old when we left for our first tour as a family, and the years we traveled together would be some of the best I've ever known. It's not that those days were easy. Parenthood is a daily mugging followed by a lotto win, the collision of theft and love, but we were together, and I got to watch my daughter grow alongside my name in lights. Kelly's burden was immense—every mother's is. She raised our girl in the back of a tour bus with little room for more than a mattress. But we held each other up, sharing every meal and moment I wasn't onstage. And when the show loaded out, I would climb into the bed beside the both of them, not believing how lucky I was.

What I do for a living borders on ridiculous. I write, I travel, and I sing for people. On a good day, I leave everything on the stage, having served my audience well. On the best days, I bear humble witness to the true power of music—how it heals and brings people together. I still feel the tension behind the keys of my piano just before the journey begins—the cocktail of fear and possibility one must weather to meet the magic on the other side. I still summon my courage and my hands in slow motion and keep my eyes closed while I'm finding my way. And if I'm lucky, I lose myself quickly, the pressure subsides, and for however long I'm up there, I get to be the pilot of a dream.

In the spring of 2015, I kicked off a festival season with my band at the Coachella polo fields outside Palm Springs. Mikey the Kid wasn't a kid anymore, but he was still holding it down on stage right with all his talent and thrift store cool. On stage left, the newest member of the band, a keyboard player named Zac Clark, was finding himself at home. In the years to come, I would lean on him as I had leaned on Josh and Raw before, but I would take his weight in return, and in a way, our connection onstage and off helped me become the leader I couldn't be for my first two bands. Finally, after ten years and everything we'd been through together, on an upstage riser sat the drummer who walked through fire with me—my copilot and my brother, JayMac. He had seen me at my worst and, like Kelly, kept his faith in me, and looking back to find him on my stage each night filled me with gratitude for the road we had traveled together. We had played those hallowed festival grounds before, but this time it was different.

The song that bore my daughter's name, "Cecilia and the Satellite," was about to break through, and as I made the long walk to my piano that April afternoon, I was ready.

The sky was cloudless cobalt and the stage a monolith on a grass field no desert should have known. Kelly wore a sleeveless yellow dress with white embroidered flowers and a wide-brimmed hat to keep her freckled cheeks safe from the sun. And while the audience watched me, I watched her…dancing with our daughter in the stage wings. The band and I climbed the walls in video, and as we did, I was delivered: from the heaviness of harder years and from a past that didn't own me any longer. The audience met me in that moment, affirming the ascent that was to follow.

Kate was in the wings with Kelly that afternoon, high school friends that time made into sisters, and somewhere in the field among the crowd were my mother and father—they never missed a show. Fatherhood had added layers to our story. My yearslong struggle and the roads it took me down awoke an empathy my youth could not supply. I would be lying to say all the walls had come down—some things don't go away. I wondered if we'd ever speak about Ohio, but it didn't haunt me like it used to. I had made it to the sun. Maybe the cemetery plot where our family tree took root was to thank for my high and healthy branches. But like the cancer, and the music, and every accident of fate along the way, my life had been extraordinary. And at some point, you have to remind yourself, when you add it all together, if you wake up where you want to be and you do what you love surrounded by people you love, maybe the pieces fell exactly as they were meant to.

Whatever came next, I had found home. A shelter for the souls to whom I'd committed everything: Kelly and Cecilia. Storms would find us there, and at least one would threaten our undoing—but we would rise to the challenge of repair. One never knows what is coming for them.

Standing on that stage, I couldn't have guessed how the chances I'd taken would change everything, but as I climbed over the barricade into a sea of dancing strangers, it was clear the future would be both glittering and weird. My name on the show poster that afternoon read, "Andrew McMahon in the Wilderness." It seemed a fitting moniker. I had spent a lifetime hunting for my truth in music and for my self-worth in the roar of a crowd, but the brilliance of that burning perfect hour was how I found both...not over my shoulders in the gathering mass but, instead, waiting for me in the wings. And if that's not wild... what *is*?

And though you were easier to fix than I was, one thing is certain, through decades, name changes, a baby, and a whole lot of healing, if someone buys a ticket with my name on it and steps into the club around nine, they'll hear the sound of my voice and the sound of yours...

♫

Acknowledgments

Lin and Brian McMahon, Emily Albanese, Chapman and Jason Retterer.
Brian Ireland, Josh Partington, Kevin Page, Reuben Hernandez,
William Tell, Bobby Anderson, Jon Sullivan, Jay and Jessie McMillan,
Mikey and Melanie Wagner, Jen Tank, Morgan Paros,
Adam and Whitney Trejo, Ryan Daniels, Bodger Millerd,
Jenny Soto-Banks, Jami Witek, Brent, Neil, and Jen Sinay, Aaron Dixon,
Andy Stensrud, Jim and Kathleen Wirt, Gary Folgner, Eric Custer,
Chris Cornell, Chris Season, J. Michael Bauer, Mike Poorman,
Alex Perkins, Chris Walkowski, Gary Schiller, Piper Walsh,
Diana Christinson, Kristina Karl, Cooper and Hamilton Karl,
Doug McMahon, Scot Delorme, Butch and Teri Witek,
Laurie and David Hansch, the Cutlip Family, the Nada Family,
the Creel-Rubinoff Family. Allison Rosenthal, Steve Smith,
Steve Mitzel, Andrea Schwartz, and everyone at Dear Jack Foundation,
Caan at the Joshua Tree Ranch House, Jon Morris and
the Windmill Factory, Jeff Johnson, Jonas Feinberg and everyone
at ZZRJ, Jake Reuter, Jonathan Daniel, Bob McLynn, and
everyone at Crush. Special thanks to Lynn Grady for her belief
and guidance, Zac Clark for his feedback and support, and to my sister
Kate for her bravery and for helping me piece it all together.
To Cecilia and Kelly, I adore you both and could not have done this
without your love. Finally, to Josh Humiston—you booked every show,
you believed, and you left too soon. I miss you brother.

Go to www.dearjackfoundation.org to learn how you can support
young adult cancer patients and survivors.

Andrew McMahon is an American singer-songwriter. He was the
vocalist and pianist for the bands Something Corporate and Jack's
Mannequin and performs solo both under his own name and under
the moniker Andrew McMahon in the Wilderness. He lives in Southern
California with his wife and daughter.